I Belong
Leader's Guide

"I have come so that they may have life and have it to the full"
(John 10:10)

redemptorist
publications

I Belong
First Holy Communion Programme

Published by **Redemptorist Publications**
Alphonsus House, Chawton, Hampshire, GU34 3HQ, UK
Tel. +44 (0)1420 88222, Fax. +44 (0)1420 88805
Email rp@rpbooks.co.uk
Web www.rpbooks.co.uk
A registered charity limited by guarantee.
Registered in England 3261721

Copyright © Redemptorist Publications, 2013

Text: Aileen Urquhart
Additional text: Yvonne Fordyce and Alison Jones

Illustrations © Finola Stack
Design: Rosemarie Pink and Emma Hagan

First Published	March 1998
Revised Publication	November 2000
Second Revised Publication	September 2010
Third Revised Publication	February 2013
Forth Revised Publication	October 2015

ISBN 978-0-85231-444-9

All rights reserved. No part of this publication may be reproduced, stored in a retrieval system, or transmitted in any form or by any means, electronic, mechanical, photocopying, recording or otherwise, without prior permission in writing from Redemptorist Publications.

Excerpts from the English translation and chants of *The Roman Missal* © 2010, International Commission on English in the Liturgy Corporation. All rights reserved.

This book is sold subject to the condition that it shall not be lent, re-sold, hired out or otherwise circulated without the publisher's prior consent in any form other than which it is published.

A CIP catalogue record for this book is available from the British Library.

Printed and bound by John Dollin Printing Services Ltd, Whitchurch, Hampshire

Dear Catechist

Welcome to **I Belong**! Whether you are an old hand at catechesis, or are just starting out on a new venture, you might be interested to know about the thinking behind this programme, and how it works in one parish.

It seems to me that spirituality, to be valid, has to be grounded in the reality in which we live. This reality is what we see, hear and touch in our daily lives, as well as the overarching reality "that no eye has seen and no ear has heard, things beyond the mind of man" (1 Corinthians 2:9). Genuine spirituality will accept both realities as white-hot heat, and find that somehow they are fused (confused seems the wrong word) and that the very dirt we walk on is holy ground indeed.

Everyday experience

This programme is therefore very much based on everyday experience, and encourages children and their parents to find the deeper realities behind everyday experiences such as eating, working and making up after a row. During each session with the parents, and then with the children, the catechists explore one of the themes.

The themes are ones that unfold naturally during the celebration of the Eucharist – such as parenthood, mercy, glory – and extra light is shed on them by looking at the Bible. But the themes start and finish with everyday experience. Hopefully, the second look at them will be enriched by everything we share about the Eucharist, the Church and the Bible during the session.

The "**Family Time**" page at the end of each chapter is designed as a review of the chapter just completed. It invites a parent and others in the family to say a prayer together; to **do** something together and to chat about the journey to the child's First Holy Communion so far.

Why do we…? What is it? What's happening? What does it mean? What's it for?

Small picture symbols will be found throughout the pages of **I Belong**. These relate to learning about: Catholic practices that have, over time, become part of Catholic worship; the people or things that one sees at Mass; words which are new to the child; and finally, the objects that one finds inside a church.

Communication

In a parish where there are several catechists it is very important to meet together regularly. Not only will you have practical details that need communicating, but more importantly you will have a wonderful opportunity to get to grips with the theme by hearing other people's insights and difficulties. After all, catechists are not "a race set apart" and the things you come up with will almost certainly be what is on the minds of the parents and children. Meeting together will make sure your catechesis is on the right wavelength and hopefully you will have an enjoyable hour or two in each other's company!

If you are working alone in a small parish you have a wonderful chance to get to know the First Communion families really well, and relating the Eucharist to what is happening in your local area will be easier than in a sprawling suburban or inner-city parish. The community aspect of the Eucharist is much more obvious when you are in a distinct community already. Paradoxically, however, you may feel that you are soldiering on alone, and it is possible that you are missing the challenge and stimulation of other catechists. Perhaps you can make contact with catechists in neighbouring parishes and compare what you are doing. Also, as said before, catechists are not a race set apart, and you could chat to anyone – family, friends, parishioners, parents of the children – about the theme in hand.

The beauty of basing the sessions on personal experience is that there are no right or wrong answers. If someone says he has never experienced the glory of God's presence, this is a valid comment. If someone says she gasps in wonder every time she sees a rainbow, this is also valid. In this instance the task of the catechist is to reach, and enable the group to reach, a greater understanding of the glory of God. Listening to one another, to what the Bible says, what the Church says, listening to the Spirit stirring within us, will bring about the understanding – an understanding of the heart more than one of the intellect.

Your own spiritual life

Of course, knowledge is necessary, so it is important to know what the Bible and the Church are saying to us. Reading the Bible prayerfully is very important to a keen catechist. The documents of Vatican II and the *Catechism of the Catholic Church* both reveal what the Church is saying. Another useful resource is the *General Directory for Catechesis*. You probably have your own selection of good spiritual writers that inspire you.

Above all, it is important to PRAY. If you are busy, and most people are these days, it is easy to put off any serious attempt at prayer, and just get by with a few quick words and a promise to "do better tomorrow". I find that tomorrow is just as busy as today, and my life is a series of promises to God. However, I still believe that prayer is the most important thing a catechist can do to improve the quality of catechesis. I am going to stop making promises to God, and actually spend some "quality" time praying now!

I hope you enjoy using **I Belong**. I hope it helps you, the team, parents and children, to grow in the love of Jesus, who is present in the consecrated bread and wine, and present in each of us. After all, this is what is at the heart of our faith, isn't it?

God bless your work.

Aileen B. Urquhart

Contents

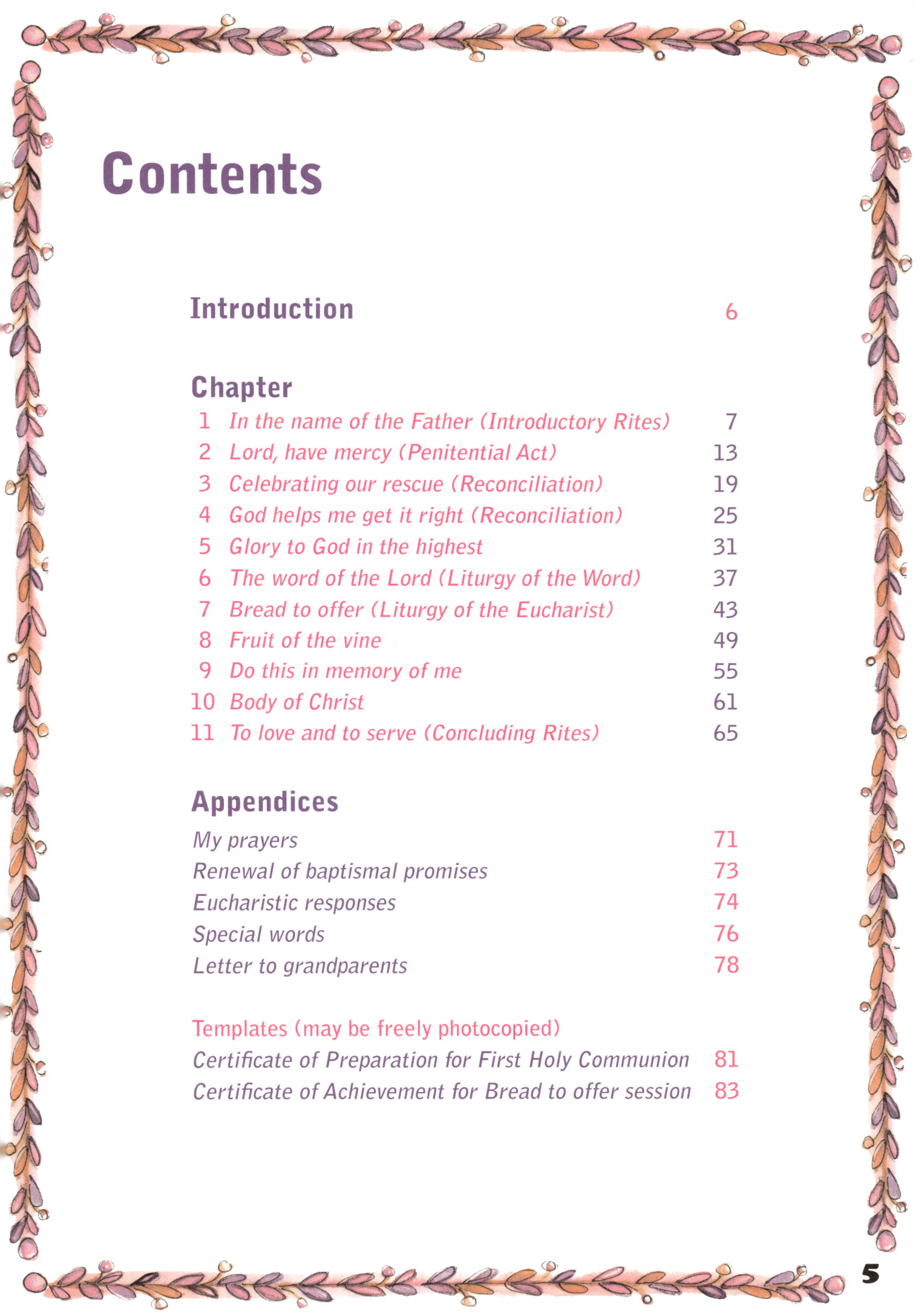

Introduction — 6

Chapter

1. *In the name of the Father (Introductory Rites)* — 7
2. *Lord, have mercy (Penitential Act)* — 13
3. *Celebrating our rescue (Reconciliation)* — 19
4. *God helps me get it right (Reconciliation)* — 25
5. *Glory to God in the highest* — 31
6. *The word of the Lord (Liturgy of the Word)* — 37
7. *Bread to offer (Liturgy of the Eucharist)* — 43
8. *Fruit of the vine* — 49
9. *Do this in memory of me* — 55
10. *Body of Christ* — 61
11. *To love and to serve (Concluding Rites)* — 65

Appendices

My prayers — 71
Renewal of baptismal promises — 73
Eucharistic responses — 74
Special words — 76
Letter to grandparents — 78

Templates (may be freely photocopied)
Certificate of Preparation for First Holy Communion — 81
Certificate of Achievement for Bread to offer session — 83

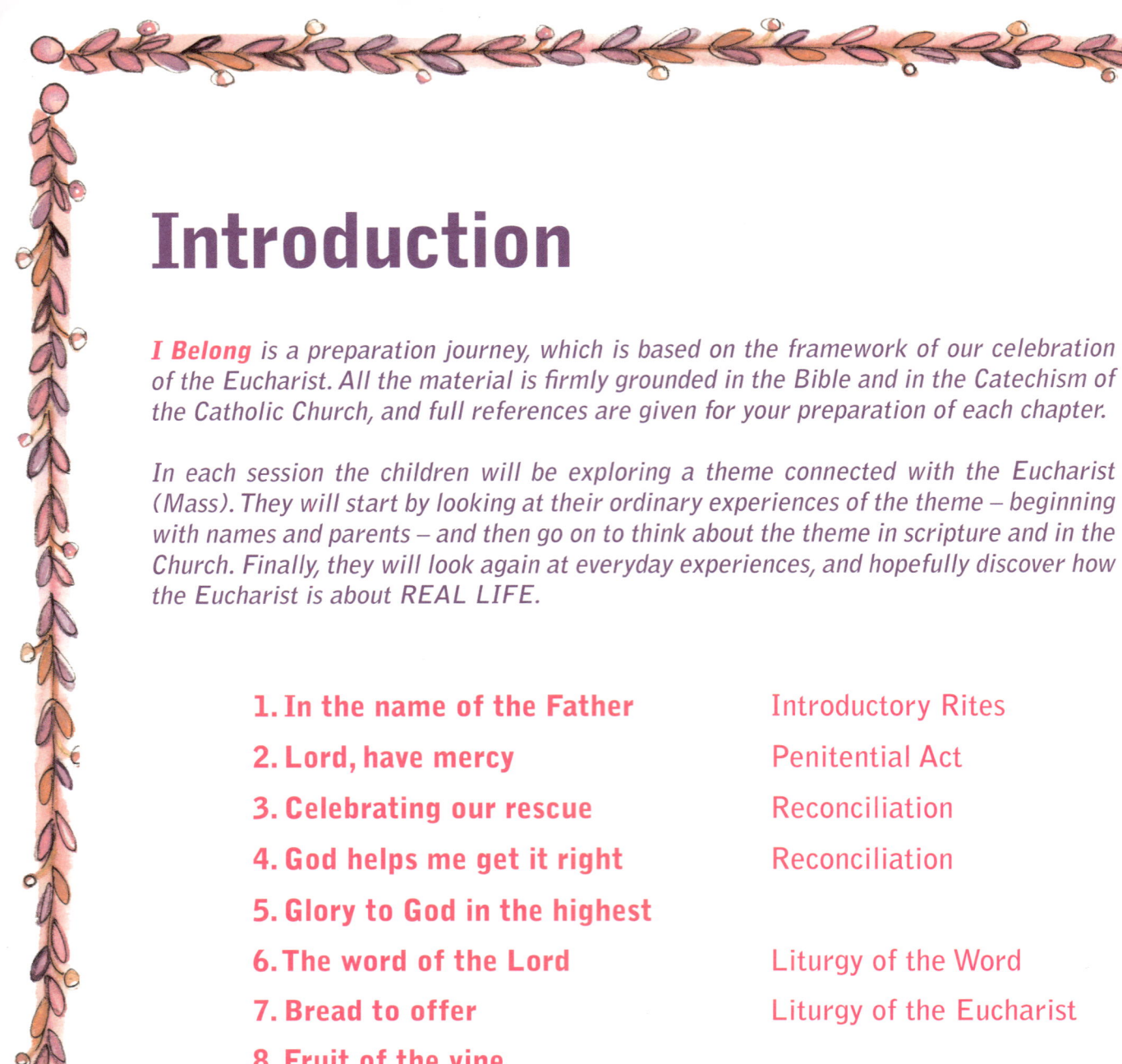

Introduction

I Belong is a preparation journey, which is based on the framework of our celebration of the Eucharist. All the material is firmly grounded in the Bible and in the Catechism of the Catholic Church, and full references are given for your preparation of each chapter.

In each session the children will be exploring a theme connected with the Eucharist (Mass). They will start by looking at their ordinary experiences of the theme – beginning with names and parents – and then go on to think about the theme in scripture and in the Church. Finally, they will look again at everyday experiences, and hopefully discover how the Eucharist is about REAL LIFE.

1. In the name of the Father	Introductory Rites
2. Lord, have mercy	Penitential Act
3. Celebrating our rescue	Reconciliation
4. God helps me get it right	Reconciliation
5. Glory to God in the highest	
6. The word of the Lord	Liturgy of the Word
7. Bread to offer	Liturgy of the Eucharist
8. Fruit of the vine	
9. Do this in memory of me	
10. Body of Christ	
11. To love and to serve	Concluding Rites

I Belong includes two chapters on reconciliation. They are complementary to any first reconciliation programme your children follow. Alternatively, the first chapters of I Belong can be adapted and developed as a separate preparation for first reconciliation, according to what you consider appropriate in your parish.

CHAPTER 1   IN THE NAME OF THE FATHER

INTRODUCTORY RITES

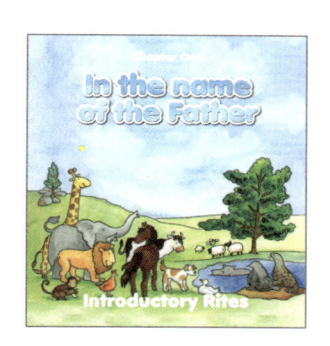

- A Bible to show the children.
- If you are running short of time, leave all colouring-in to be done at home.
- If you have time left over, colour in the picture on page 7, practise the sign of the cross and the Our Father.

Page 2 Church

An introduction to the key themes of First Holy Communion. Spend some time practising the sign of the cross with the children.

■ **Parent's book** An introduction to your church and the sign of the cross. You might want to practise this at home with your child.

Page 3 Exploring "names" in a child's everyday life experience

Take plenty of time over this. Get the children to tell each other their friends' names and take the opportunity to learn theirs. Have fun listening to one another's ideas for pets' names.

References: Isaiah 43:1 (called by name), John 10:3 (sheep know the voice), Catechism of the Catholic Church 2156-2167 (importance of names in Christianity).

■ **Parent's book** The names we are called can affect us deeply. You probably spent a long time choosing a name for your child. It had to be just right. You may also remember suffering as a child if you were constantly called names such as "lazybones", or heard your parents label you in some way or another.

Pages 4 to 5 The Old Testament

Show the children the Bible and how it is divided into two sections. Show them the beginning, where the creation story is. Discuss what animals the children will draw. They could put them in a jungle, forest, garden or zoo setting.

Discuss with them what a king is, what a judge is, what a parent is. Remember, we're talking about NAMES.

References: Genesis 2:19-20 (Adam names animals), Gaudium et spes 12 (people made in the image of God).

7

■ **Parent's book** In scripture, the use of names is often very significant. Adam (the name means "of the earth") represents all of us, men and women alike. The link with earth is not to be despised. Creation is glorious. Genesis tells us that God saw creation was good… good… very good. Adam's naming of the animals means that we have power and, therefore, responsibility over the rest of creation.

Pages 5 to 6 The New Testament

Show the children where the New Testament begins in a bible. In the annunciation we learn that Jesus is the Son of God and the Son of Mary. Concentrate on the baptism of Our Lord and his experience of being a beloved son.

References: Luke 1:31-32 (annunciation), Matthew 3:13-17 (baptism of Christ – Son revealed by the Father), Catechism of the Catholic Church 238-240 (Father revealed by the Son), Catechism of the Catholic Church 430-438 (names of "Jesus" and "Christ"), Gaudium et spes 22 (Christ the new man).

■ **Parent's book** At the annunciation God became part of this glorious creation, thus making it even more magnificent. By becoming human God became subject to other human beings, and was also **named.** The name Jesus (Joshua) means **saviour**.

In the **Old Testament**, Joshua was the one who led the Israelites over the River Jordan into the freedom of the Promised Land after their forty years in the desert. It was not by accident that Jesus was baptised in the Jordan. He is the true Joshua, leading us all to fulfilment and life. The baptism of Jesus also has links with the story of creation. Just as in **Genesis** the Spirit of God hovered over the waters of chaos and brought forth life, so the Spirit hovered over Jesus. Jesus is the **second Adam** – the new creation. In Adam, we walk in friendship with God. In Jesus, we are re-created as children of God.

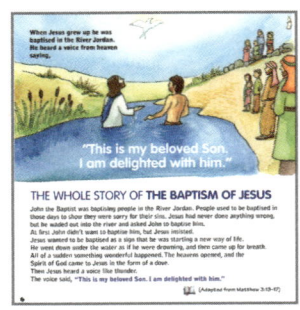

Page 8 Church

Some children may have been to a baptism recently. Discuss with them what they see at a baptism, especially the pouring of the water.

Stress the link between what the Father said to Jesus and what God said to them when they were baptised. God is their father as well, and is delighted with them. Stress the similarities between their baptism and Jesus' baptism (God's love, indwelling of the Spirit, new way of living).

Note: Be sensitive when discussing fathers: some children may have bad experiences, or may not live with their father.

Discuss where the holy water is in the church. Some of them may have been to a Mass when holy water was sprinkled on the people. This too reminds us of our baptism.

The children might like to sing the Our Father if they are not too shy.

References: Catechism of the Catholic Church 535-537 (links between Christ's baptism and ours), Catechism of the Catholic Church 1265-1267 (new creature incorporated into Church/body of Christ).

■ **Parent's book** For Jesus, his baptism was a powerful sign of his sonship. In baptism, we are saying many things. We are not only celebrating the new life – the new **Adam** – that has been brought into the world, but also joining Jesus in his relationship with his Father. Baptism is the Spirit breathing life into the chaos; it is the crossing over the waters of the Jordan into a new life of liberty; it is God calling us his beloved children. It is our baptism that gives us the right to come together as the Church. It unites us all as children of God: all equal, all loved.

Page 9 *Everyday Life*

This section is about everyday life. It could also serve as an introduction to the sacrament of reconciliation. Keep it very positive. Don't dwell on the children's possible failings. Stress that we have the power to live like Jesus.

The word search uses words that describe a loving parent. Ask the children why those words have been used.

References: Romans 6:1-4 (baptised into death of Christ, new life), Lumen gentium 39 (called to holiness), Catechism of the Catholic Church 2012-2013 (Christian holiness).

■ **Parent's book** It would be wonderful to be constantly aware of our dignity as children of God. So often we put ourselves down: "**Oh, I'm so stupid**," "**Oh, you are a nuisance**." Perhaps we could start saying good things about ourselves and others. We are all God's beloved children.

At home you might like to go through the **Our Father** with your child, explaining some of the more difficult words. If you don't already say night prayers together this could be a good time to start. You could also talk about his or her baptism. If you had a party at the time, tell your child about it. Much of the scripture that we will be looking at during the next few months will mention parties and celebrations, and it will all be leading up to the celebration of your child's **First Holy Communion**.

Page 10 *Family Time*

■ **Parent's book** Choose a place where you can talk about this page with your child and any other family member. Think about the special words you have met in this chapter. Did you find the baptismal font in your church?

Perhaps light a candle and say the prayer together.

Encourage your child to use his or her book. Colour the flame of the candle on the top right-hand corner of each page where there is one as you go through the book.

Certificate to go with the service on page 12. The template can be found at the back of the book.

This is to say that I

_____

_____

am preparing for my
FIRST HOLY COMMUNION

~

I will do my best to attend all the sessions, and with God's help I will grow more like JESUS every day.

PARENTS' SESSION

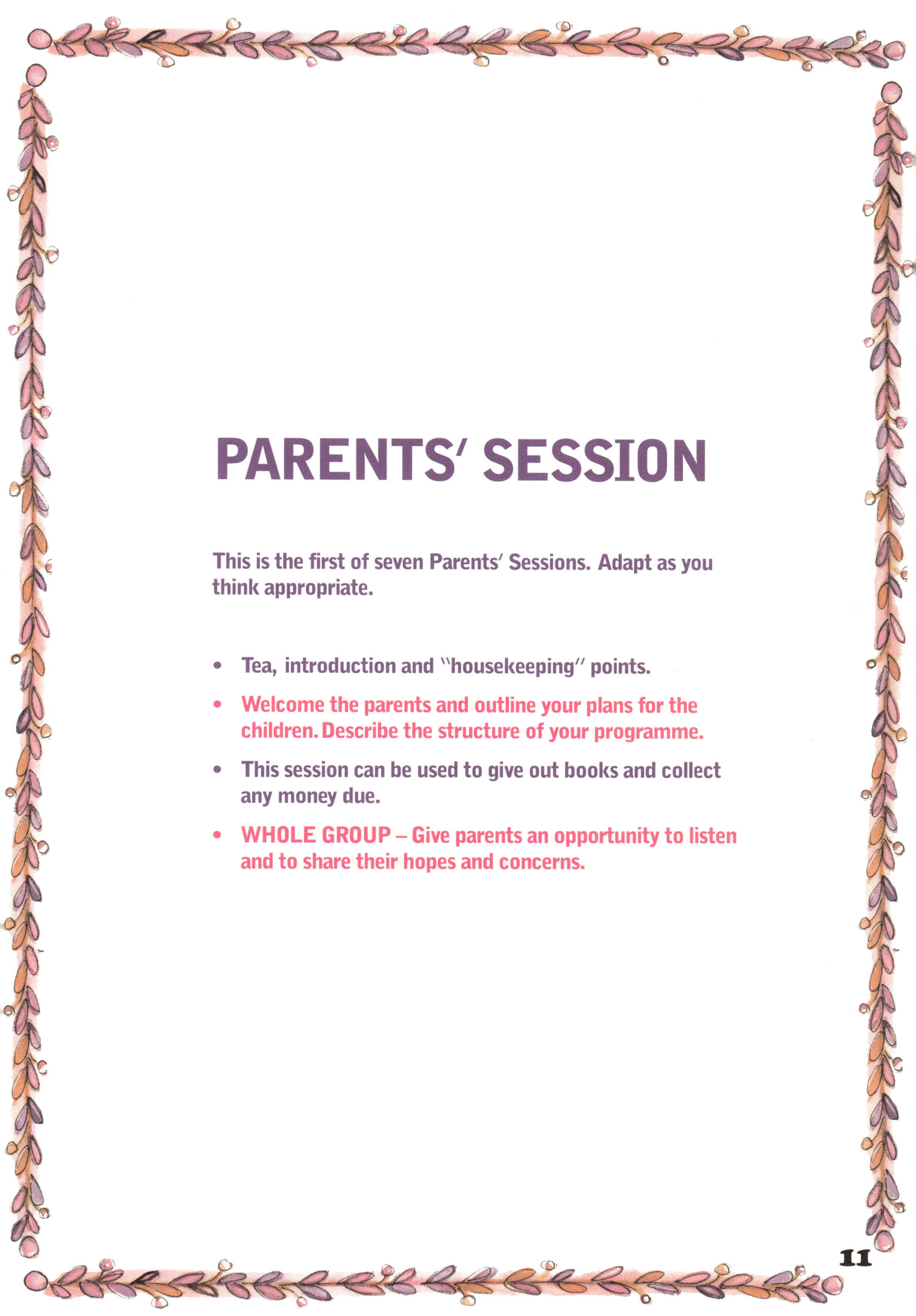

This is the first of seven Parents' Sessions. Adapt as you think appropriate.

- **Tea, introduction and "housekeeping" points.**
- **Welcome the parents and outline your plans for the children. Describe the structure of your programme.**
- **This session can be used to give out books and collect any money due.**
- **WHOLE GROUP – Give parents an opportunity to listen and to share their hopes and concerns.**

SERVICE *In the name of the Father*

You will need:

- **The cast: angel Gabriel, Mary**
- **Certificates of enrolment**
- **Shawl for Mary**
- **Alb for Gabriel**

Opening Prayer

Father in heaven, you love us so much and you know all our names because we are your children. Today we have been thinking about names, and how important they are. We have learnt about Adam naming the animals and caring for them. We have learnt about the baptism of Jesus when he was grown up. Help us to listen to the full story of how Jesus got his name before he was born. We ask this through Jesus Christ, your Son.
Amen.

Gospel: Luke 1:26-38

The angel Gabriel was sent from God to a city of Galilee named Nazareth, to a virgin who was going to marry a man called Joseph, of the house of David. The virgin's name was Mary. The angel said to Mary, "Hail, full of grace, the Lord is with you." But she was greatly troubled when the angel said this, and wondered what the angel meant. "Don't be afraid, Mary," said the angel, "for God loves you very much. You will have a baby, and you shall call him Jesus. He will be great, and will be called the Son of the Most High. He will reign for ever, and his kingdom will never end." Mary said to the angel, "How can this happen? I haven't got a husband." The angel said, "The Holy Spirit will come upon you, and the child will be called holy, the Son of God." Mary said, "I am the Lord's handmaid. Let it all happen as you said."

Two children to act out the story… (1) angel Gabriel, (2) Mary.

Reflection

God knows each of you by name. Because of your baptism you are children of God. He is your Father. The next stage is Holy Communion. This year the First Holy Commuion group will prepare for this.

Children to come up in pairs for their certificate (for them to fill in at home).

Minister: Please take this certificate of enrolment.
Child: Thank you.

Prayer

Father, we know you love us very much. Thank you for sending Jesus to us. Thank you for the gift of baptism. Help us during the coming year as we prepare for our First Holy Communion. We ask this…

CHAPTER 2   LORD, HAVE MERCY
PENITENTIAL ACT

- There is plenty of material in the book. Take your time to chat to the children. It is good if children DON'T finish the section in the book, as it gives them something to do at home with their families.
- Don't forget to check that the previous session's work has been finished.

■ **Parent's book** In this session the children will be thinking about **mercy** in everyday life, scripture and the Church. Hopefully they will come to a better understanding of the mercy of God, and how we are called to be merciful in our day-to-day dealings with people. At the Eucharist, we come before our loving God to receive infinite mercy, and are challenged and empowered to pass on this gift so freely and lovingly given.

Pages 12 to 13 Everyday Life

In the story, the child is like God to the kitten. (Usually children are like the kitten – at the receiving end.) Encourage the children to come up with suitable God-like attitudes of caring and mercy. The picture could be their family kissing, cuddling or playing together.

References: Mass: Kyrie, Agnus Dei; Psalm 103 and Isaiah 63:7-9 (mercy of God), Romans 5:12-21 (where sin increased, grace abounded all the more), Catechism of the Catholic Church 270 (God's mercy), Catechism of the Catholic Church 2447 (works of mercy).

■ **Parent's book** Children are completely dependent on the merciful love of adults. Their concept of mercy will depend on the experience of mercy that they have received from **US**. God is traditionally portrayed as a father. A child's picture of God will be based on the parenting they receive from **US**. If we forgive them willingly, and forget past bad behaviour, they will grow up with confidence in life, and in the God who gives us life.

Page 14 The Old Testament

Remind children of the previous session. Then find an opportunity to discuss with your fellow catechists and priest what to say if a child asks why there is STILL evil in the world: the age-old problem of evil and suffering. No pat answer, but most human beings have a basic HOPE in life, truth and goodness. We believe that ultimately good triumphs over bad. As Christians our FAITH and HOPE are founded on Jesus.

References: Genesis 3:15 (first promise of the Redeemer), Gaudium et spes 13 (human condition/redemption), Catechism of the Catholic Church 407-412 (sin/redemption "happy fault").

■ **Parent's book** The creation stories in the Bible were written down about 800 BC but some parts are much older. King David had united the tribes into one kingdom and there was relative peace and prosperity. People had time to think about the meaning of life, and other big questions such as the problem of suffering and evil. Under the inspiration of God, **Genesis** was written. What it contains is not **scientific** truth but **theological** truth. The story of the serpent and the forbidden fruit acknowledges that, although wonderfully created, we all struggle with the temptation to do evil. However, this basic weakness of ours is the opportunity for God's wonderful mercy towards us, in the promise of a Saviour. Every year during the Easter Vigil we hear the sin of Adam called a "**happy fault**".

Pages 15 to 16 The New Testament

The story of the Prodigal Son is one of Jesus' many wonderful stories, maybe the best known! Discuss the feelings of all characters involved. Stress the PARTY aspect of the homecoming.

References: Luke 15:1-32 (lost sheep, lost coin, lost son), Gaudium et spes 45 (Christ Alpha and Omega), Catechism of the Catholic Church 388-390 (Christian understanding of the fall).

■ **Parent's book** We will be looking closely at the story of the **Prodigal Son** during the parents' sessions. There is a bit of each character in all of us. We can in turn be the forgiving father, the tearaway younger son and the self-righteous elder brother. A good book on this is **The Return of the Prodigal Son** by Henri Nouwen.

Page 18 Church

It's worth remembering that the younger son's motives for returning weren't particularly praiseworthy, but that didn't matter. The joy of the father was so strong it blotted out everything else and the son was swept up in the reunion. We go to church with all sorts of negative feelings – the children may be bored or at odds with their "elder brothers" – but God IS ALWAYS FULL OF LOVE. We are cared for and tended with infinitely merciful love. Emphasise the connection between the younger son's homecoming party and the Eucharist. They will be receiving special food next year to celebrate the fact that no matter how far away we wander, God is always waiting there for us.

References: Luke 18:13 (mercy on me, a sinner), Eucharistic Prayer IV (God's redemptive action in history), Catechism of the Catholic Church 2629-2631 (prayer of petition for mercy).

■ **Parent's book** We say "**Lord, have mercy**" – *Kyrie, eleison* – at the Eucharist. Some scholars say the word *eleison* comes from the word for olive. The **mercy** we receive from God is like the olive twig, a symbol of hope, which the dove brought to Noah when the flood waters subsided. We can imagine the prodigal son being freshly bathed and anointed with oil of the olives before he put on the new robes, sandals and ring. We are reminded of the anointing of priests and kings in the Bible, and of our own anointing as holy and royal people at our baptism. This rich abundance is what we expect from God when we ask for **mercy**. Read **School for Prayer** by Archbishop Anthony Bloom for more about this.

Page 19 *Everyday Life*

Acknowledge children's negative feelings when they are hurt. This is the reality. Our feelings can be useful signals to us that something is wrong and we must take some action to put things right. Because we are NOT God it is hard to do the right (merciful) thing. Every time we DO show mercy we are becoming more God-like. Health warning! We are NOT encouraging the children to become doormats. Mercy is something that only those with power can give. Also, it is more than just refraining from punishing: it is positive.

See Shakespeare: *"The quality of mercy is not strained… It is twice blest: it blesseth him that gives and him that takes."*
The Merchant of Venice, Act IV, Scene I

Emphasise God's mercy, rather than our need for mercy. The parents have entrusted their children to us, and we must not destroy their self-esteem.

References: Isaiah 58:6-7 (the fast God requires), Hosea 6:6 (mercy, not sacrifice), Our Father (forgive as we forgive), Catechism of the Catholic Church 2447 (works of mercy).

■ **Parent's book** There is a playground game called "**Mercy, Mercy**" in which one child squeezes another child's finger until he or she cries for mercy. This is not what we mean by mercy. We mean something altogether more positive, more like an aromatherapy massage. Shakespeare puts it like this:

"The quality of mercy is not strained; it droppeth as the gentle rain from heaven upon the place beneath. It is twice blest: it blesseth him that gives and him that takes. 'Tis mightiest in the mightiest; it becomes the throned monarch better than his crown… It is enthroned in the hearts of kings, it is an attribute of God himself."
The Merchant of Venice, Act IV, Scene I

Page 20 *Family Time*

■ **Parent's book** Choose a place where you can talk about this page with your child and any other family member.
Do the word search together and discuss the words chosen.
You may like to light a candle and say the prayer together.
In the space on this page, help your child think about a prayer **he** or **she** could write.

PARENTS' SESSION

Adapt as you think appropriate.

- **Modern music evocative of the theme of mercy/leaving home and the like.**

- **Tea/welcome and "housekeeping" points.**

- **In groups, discuss how the father, prodigal son and elder brother felt when:**

    (a) the younger son left

    and

    (b) the younger son came home

- **WHOLE GROUP** – draw the discussion to an end.

- **If there is time to spare, do "brainstorming" on the word "mercy", but it may be a good idea to finish with an appropriate poem, as in the past it has been a moving, thought-provoking climax to the session.**

SERVICE *Lord, have mercy*

You will need:

- The cast: father, son, elder brother, partygoers, pigs, servants
- Mix lavender oil and base oil in a container with cotton wool on the side

Hymn
Oh, the love of my Lord – *Verses 1 and 2*

Opening Prayer
Father, we have been learning about your merciful love.
We have spoken about the story in our session.
Now help us to understand it better by acting out the story.
We ask this through Christ our Lord, who was the first person to tell this story.
Amen.
Children to come forward and act out the story as it is read out to them.

Gospel: Luke 15:11-32
The prodigal son.

Reflection
Remind the children of what the focus of the service is (draw conclusions from them).
We are like the prodigal son when we don't act as children of God.
We come to our senses when we start behaving like God's children, and God always welcomes us, and we come up smelling of roses!
Children come up for anointing on the forehead by the minister.
Minister: Always remember you are a beloved child of God.
Child: I will.

Prayer
Father, we thank you that you are always looking out for us with love. We thank you for your merciful love. We thank you that no matter how silly or unkind we have been, you still love us and we are still your children. Help us always to act as beloved children, because that is what we are. We ask this through Jesus Christ, our Lord.
Amen.

Hymn
Oh, the love of my Lord – *Verse 3*

NOTES

CHAPTER 3   CELEBRATING OUR RESCUE
RECONCILIATION

This is our first session on the sacrament of reconciliation. For whatever reason, some children can become confused or even anxious when this sacrament is raised. Please do stress to the children that, apart from anything else, EVERY sacrament is a CELEBRATION of God's unconditional care for us. The sacrament of reconciliation is no different. Today we are looking at reconciliation as God's act of rescue; next time we will look at reconciliation as God's act of changing us for the better. We will look at this next time when we see how Zacchaeus changed after meeting Jesus.

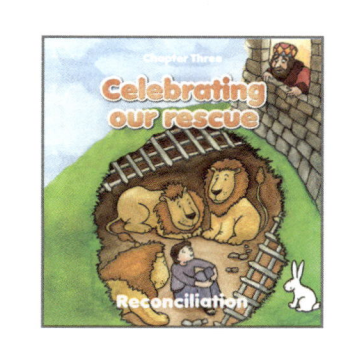

■ **Parent's book** This is the first of two sessions to help the children prepare for their first reconciliation. At the next session, they will be thinking about how God helps them "**get it right**" and how reconciliation can give us help for the future. To begin with, though, they will be thinking of how we are always being rescued by God. Reconciliation is always taking place in everyday life, and the sacrament of reconciliation is an opportunity to praise God for God's understanding, help and forgiveness in the past.

Pages 22 to 24 *Everyday life*

Page 23 is meant to show how dramatic rescuing can be. The rescuer is often in danger him- or herself! Look at what Jesus went through to rescue us! Also, stress the relief and joy after a rescue. Everyone celebrates. The idea is to link their own relief/joy at finding something dear to them with God's joy when we return to the fold. ("More joy over one sinner who repents, than ninety-nine righteous people" – end of lost sheep parable, Luke 15.)

■ **Parent's book** You could remind your child of any rescue he or she has seen. Maybe a road accident or fire. Perhaps your child tried to rescue a bird fallen out of a tree, or stood up for a younger child who was being bullied. If your child has ever been lost, you could discuss how he or she felt. (The odds are **YOU** were even more worried than the child was! Use this as an illustration of how pleased God is when we are back on the right path.)

   What we need to get across to the children is **that they are basically GOOD, and that sometimes they lose their way and need** "**rescuing**". We are not trying to say that they are sinful and need constant correcting, in order that they will occasionally be good and lovable.

Page 25 *The Old Testament*

I think this story and the next one should be read by a catechist unless you have very good readers in your group. Also, an adult can lend a dramatic quality to the stories which children are not able to do.

It is worth reading this story (Daniel 6) before the children's session as it is very rich in meaning. Daniel says he was rescued because he trusted. Also, King Darius' nationwide proclamation is so prophetic. It is a real declaration of faith in an eternal God who "saves and rescues".

References: Daniel 6 (story of Daniel), Daniel 6:25-27 (King Darius' act of faith in the God who saves), Daniel 3:19-30 (three men in furnace – another example of God as saviour), Psalm 36 (our sinfulness and the mercy of God), Psalm 69 (cry for help).

■ **Parent's book** In the past, our picture of God has sometimes been distorted. Because people have seen God as all-holy and perfect, they have stressed the distance between God and human beings, and dwelt on our sinfulness and unworthiness. This is true but must be balanced by the image of God as a loving parent, and ourselves as made in the image and likeness of God. God is Emmanuel – God with us. **"Does a mother forget her baby...Yet even if these forget, I will never forget you"** (Isaiah 49:15).

Page 26 *The New Testament*

Shepherds had a dangerous job in those days living out in the wilds and with ferocious beasts to contend with. Notice the celebration at the end of the parable given in Luke 15:4-7. This is a "model" of reconciliation. We are helpless: it is God who does the saving. "Without me you can do nothing."

References: Luke 15:4-7 (lost sheep), Matthew 16:18-19 (you are Peter), Catechism of the Catholic Church 1444 (power of the keys to Peter).

■ **Parent's book** The parable of the lost sheep is one of three parables: the lost sheep, the lost coin, the prodigal son, all placed together in Luke's Gospel, about God's joy over returning sinners. They are three stories told to some self-righteous scribes and Pharisees who were disgusted at Jesus because he mixed with "publicans and sinners". To those Jews who kept every purity law, even those laws that were only to be observed by priests before offering sacrifice in the Temple, anyone who could not, because of their job for instance, was considered by them to be a sinner.

Page 28 *Everyday Life*

Feelings are neither good nor bad, they are signals that let us know what is going on. It is what we DO with our feelings that can be good or bad. Try to keep it positive, and think of all the times the children "get it right". Even if they have been really naughty, they have come through it and are still loved by their family and others. Stress that just as their parents still love them, no matter what they do, so does God to an even greater extent. We might fail but God never does.

■ **Parent's book** The children will be thinking about feelings, and how they are useful signals to their needs. At home you are shepherds to your children when you empathise with their anger, hurt, envy and so on, and rescue them by helping them find good ways of dealing with their problems. **NEVER SAY TO YOUR CHILD, "I WON'T LOVE/LIKE YOU IF…"** Apart from being a devastating statement, it is not a reflection of God's parenthood. GOD IS LOVE.

Page 29 *Church*

(Links everyday life with the sacrament.) Stress the CELEBRATION. Reassure them about the secrecy of reconciliation. You might like to discuss the sorts of things that they might say in reconciliation. Things done by accident, no matter how awful the consequences, are not sins. Sins are to do with deliberately damaging your relationship with God and others, or damaging yourself.

References: Catechism of the Catholic Church 1440-1498 (chapter on the sacrament of reconciliation) including 1441-1442 (only God forgives sins – apostolic ministry of the sacrament of reconciliation), 1447 (history of the sacrament of reconciliation over the centuries), 1467 (sacramental seal, secrecy of confessional), Code of Canon Law 983 (sacramental seal).

■ **Parent's book** Because Catholics have often inherited a tendency to stress the distance between God and us, reconciliation has sometimes been seen as something very negative. Try to stress the **celebration** aspect with your child. We are celebrating God's forgiving love and ongoing help.

Page 30 Introduction to the theme of the next chapter

Reconciliation also equips us for the future.

Reference: Catechism of the Catholic Church 1468-1469 (effects of sacrament: conciliation with self, God, Church, all creation).

Page 31

A much harder word search. Hope it is not too difficult.

Page 32 Family Time

■ **Parent's book** Choose a place where you can talk about this page with your child and any other family member. Think about "thank you" prayers and help each other to write one. Talk about the loving and kind things that we can do for one another. You may like to draw the pictures together.

After Mass one Sunday, or on a separate visit, search your church for the two places described on this page.

SERVICE   *Celebrating our rescue*

You will need:
- **The cast: good shepherd, lost sheep, other sheep**
- **Plasters, preferably with pictures on them**

Hymn
Oh, the love of my Lord

Opening Prayer
Heavenly Father, you look after us every minute of our lives, and care for us every moment of every day. You are still with us when we get into danger.
Thank you for loving us so much, and help us to love you too.
We ask this through Jesus Christ, our Lord.
Amen.

*Children to come forward and act out the story as it is read out to them.
Good shepherd, lost sheep, other sheep.*

Gospel: Luke 15:4-7
The lost sheep.

Reflection
About times children were in danger, lost or found, and the love of God.
Children come up for plasters…
Catechist: Next time you are hurt, remember God is with you.
Child: I will.

Prayer
Heavenly Father, thank you for your great love for us, which never changes no matter what we do or where we go. Help us to be full of love too, and rescue us from evil, so everyone will know we are your children.
We ask this through Jesus Christ, our Lord.
Amen.

Hymn
Give me joy in my heart

NOTES

CHAPTER 4   GOD HELPS ME GET IT RIGHT
RECONCILIATION

■ **Parent's book** At our last session we thought about how God rescues us from past failings, and how reconciliation is going on in life all the time. We go to the sacrament of reconciliation to CELEBRATE God's forgiving love. In this session we are still thinking about celebrating, but with a focus on the future. When we CONFIDE in the priest we are CONFIDENT that the sacrament gives us help for the times we "**get it wrong**".

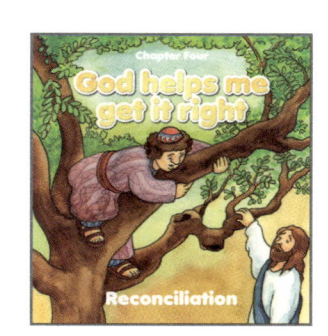

Pages 35 to 36 *Everyday Life*

This part is mostly discussion and drawing. It is worth remembering how painful it is when we get things wrong: how hard it is to BE wrong. The children may not want to admit to anything that made them feel inadequate. When they get things right it might be hard for them to acknowledge that they were helped! These tendencies are one of the reasons why people find it so hard to go to confession. Also, we often have bad experiences of saying sorry in our everyday lives. People can be unforgiving, or have very long memories: "I forgive but I can't forget!" God's love is so different from this. God forgives instantly, and there is no past with God, just one loving present.

References: Gaudium et spes 15-16 (dignity of intellect/moral conscience). NB There are no Old Testament references in this children's session, but you might like to reflect on the following passages which illustrate God helping people "get it right": 2 Samuel 11-12 (David's sin and his repentance after Nathan's parable), book of Jonah (Jonah learns of God's universal love and forgiveness).

■ **Parent's book** Remind the children about achievements like learning to swim, riding a bike and reading a book. A lot of mistakes went into each process, but you were there to encourage and help. It is probably your experience that any time you were impatient or uninterested in their struggles they did not do very well, and even shrivelled up a bit. But when you gave your wholehearted attention to their struggle they seemed to blossom. God is the good parent, who encourages us even when we fail. God's belief in us gives us the courage to believe in ourselves. God says, "Go on, I know you can do it," and we find it is true.

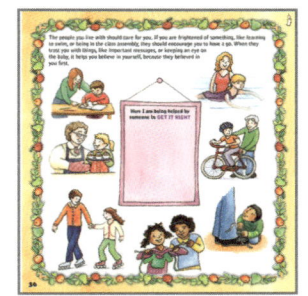

25

Pages 37 to 38 The New Testament: Zacchaeus

References: Prodigal son, Luke 15:11-32 (children looked at this story in the second session), the lost sheep, Luke 15:4-7 (children looked at this story in the previous session), Luke 19:1-10 (Zacchaeus, the man Jesus helped "get it right"), Luke 19:8 (reference to Exodus 21:37, the Jewish law of restitution), John 8:11 ("Go... don't sin any more").

■ **Parent's book** The children have had two parables about forgiveness already – the prodigal son and the lost sheep. Each story ends with a party – a celebration that what was lost is now found. They are now hearing about a real-life situation when Jesus "practises what he preaches". Jesus searches out the lost son of Abraham, and the celebration itself brings about the wonderful transformation in Zacchaeus.

Zacchaeus, the tax collector, was a collaborator with the Roman authorities, so was considered a traitor by the "decent" people. Tax collectors collected the money that the Romans exacted; but they were allowed to collect any amount they liked and they usually pocketed the difference. It was this man whom Jesus singled out to dine with. The effect on Zacchaeus was remarkable. Having been affirmed by Jesus, he confessed his guilt and decided to make amends. His offer to pay back four times what he had wrongly taken was a direct reference to the Jewish law – he was acting as a good Jew now, not as a public sinner, for, as Jesus said of him, "This man too is a son of Abraham." The message for us is: if we treat our children as sons and daughters of God they will act like sons and daughters of God.

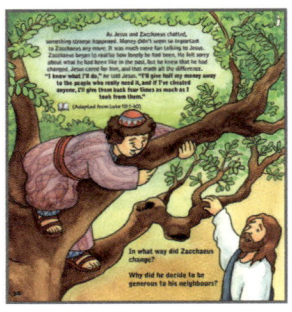

Pages 40 to 42 The Sacrament

You may well go off at a tangent on this page. Answer the children's questions and put their minds at rest about reconciliation. Keep linking it back to the stories of the prodigal son, the lost sheep and Zacchaeus. All ended with a celebration. There was nothing judgemental in any of the stories. Zacchaeus was able to change because Jesus affirmed him. Children (and adults) will live up to what is expected of them. Stress the secrecy of reconciliation. Priests never tell what they hear.

References: Catechism of the Catholic Church 1467 (secrecy of confession), Catechism of the Catholic Church 1480-1482 (the elements of the sacrament of reconciliation), Sacrosanctum concilium 26-27 (liturgical services and administration of sacraments), Catechism of the Catholic Church 1490 (past and future aspects of reconciliation).

■ **Parent's book** These pages have a lot of reading for the children, and in their sessions with the catechists they will not have time to discuss all the points. Please go through them with your child, so he or she is quite confident as to what reconciliation is all about. You will notice that the emphasis is very positive. We are thanking God for God's forgiveness, and asking help for the future. God really does believe in us (we are made in God's image after all!) and says to us, as Jesus said to the woman taken in adultery, "**Go... don't sin any more.**"

Page 42 *What happens?*

The mechanics of reconciliation. If the children know what to expect it is less daunting for them.

Page 44 *Family Time*

- Your child will be familiar with these words by now. Talk about them with all the family. Allow your child the pleasure of showing everyone his or her work and give the child due support and encouragement.

PARENTS' SESSION

Arrange to provide tea, coffee and biscuits.

In groups

Tell the group about something you found difficult to do at first, but how in the end you were helped to get it right. If you were given an Oscar for it, who would you have to thank in your speech? What experiences has your child had of reinforcing the message that we don't have to "go it alone"?

Possible points for discussion

- What made Jesus want to eat with Zacchaeus rather than with the law-abiding Jews?

- What were Zacchaeus' values before and after meeting Jesus?

- What made Zacchaeus change?

- Have you ever felt that God is with you, helping you with personal shortcomings?

- How do you think that you could get most benefit from the sacrament of reconciliation?

- What can we do to encourage our children to see the sacrament of reconciliation as a joyful expression of our belief that God helps us to "get it right"?

SERVICE   God helps me get it right

You will need:
- Cast: Jesus, Zacchaeus, crowd
- Recorded music
- Plants for tree
- Children's pictures of themselves getting it right/being kind
- Stickers with "God helps me 'get it right'" written on them

Hymn
Oh, the love of my Lord

(an opportunity to practise for the sacrament of reconciliation, if appropriate)

Opening Prayer
Heavenly Father, you sent your Son Jesus to show us how to live and love.
Help us to realise how much you love us as we prepare for our first reconciliation.
We ask this through your Son, Jesus Christ our Lord. Amen.

Gospel: Luke 19:1-10 (Zacchaeus)
Children to act it out while Gospel is read.

Reflection
On the theme of God helps us to "get it right".
Jesus believed in Zacchaeus, so he lived up to Jesus' expectations.

Children process with pictures of themselves getting something right, for example playing nicely. Catechists take the pictures and give the children a sticker with "God helps me to 'get it right'" on it.

Sign of Peace

Prayer
Father, we thank you that you are always looking out for us with love. We thank you for your merciful love. We thank you that, no matter how silly or unkind we have been, you still love us and we are still your children. Help us always to act as beloved children, because that is what we are. We ask this through Jesus Christ, our Lord. Amen.

Hymn
God forgave my sin

(an opportunity to practise for the sacrament of reconciliation, if appropriate)

NOTES

CHAPTER 5   GLORY TO GOD IN THE HIGHEST

Consider starting this session with a five to ten minute excerpt from the classic film *ET* (chosen for its GLORIOUS/WONDERFUL quality).

- **Parent's book** In this session the children will be thinking about **GLORY**. This is a difficult concept, but a very important one. Everything Jesus did was for the **GLORY** of his Father, and to follow in his footsteps all our actions should also be for the **HONOUR** and **GLORY** of God.

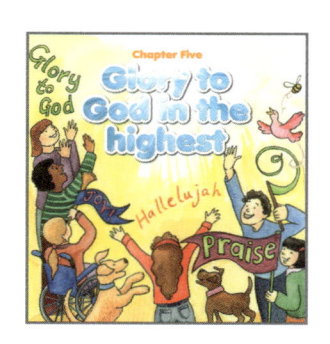

Page 46 *Everyday Life*

Straightforward examples and discussion. If they talk about the danger of fireworks this could be quite good. God is not a tame pussycat! (Children may know of Aslan in *The Lion, the Witch and the Wardrobe*.)

References: Isaiah 6:1-5 (Isaiah's vision), Catechism of the Catholic Church 2809 (glory of God/humanity).

- **Parent's book** The children may not have had many experiences of actually receiving **GLORY**, but they may well have had experiences which leave them gasping with wonder. A magnificent fireworks display, or the first time they saw snow are two possibilities among thousands.

Pages 48 to 49 *The Old Testament*

You need to know the story of Moses as a baby in case the children ask you. The story is in Exodus 1 and 2. (Burning bush is in Exodus 3.) Some catechists have found that it is better if THEY read the stories in the children's books rather than the children. That way the children can concentrate on the meaning of the story, rather than on deciphering the words.

References: Exodus 3:1-10 (burning bush), Catechism of the Catholic Church 203-209 (God reveals his name).

- **Parent's book** The **GLORY** (*shekinah*) of God is spoken of again and again in the Old Testament. In the burning bush episode we learn that we cannot name God **(I Am who I Am)** for God is utterly beyond us.

   However, we learn that this **HOLY GOD** is a God who **SAVES**. God led the slaves through the desert to freedom, the ***shekinah*** remaining with them as a pillar of fire by night, and of cloud by day.

   St Irenaeus said, "**The glory of God is a human being fully alive.**" This is seen most powerfully in Jesus, but the glory of God is also shining in each one of us. We and our children are burning bushes. When we approach one another we approach holy ground. Let us teach our children to reverence the holiness of others. To love God and to love our neighbour are two sides of the same coin.

Pages 49 to 50 The New Testament

There are many different ways we see God's glory. It is important to stress the **quiet glory** of the manger, because of the **quiet glory** of the Eucharist. When they acknowledge Jesus under the forms of bread and wine, they are like the shepherds acknowledging God in the baby in Bethlehem. The difference is that for the shepherds, only the divinity of Christ was hidden. For us, the humanity of Christ is also hidden.

References: Luke 2:8-20 (shepherds hear Good News), Catechism of the Catholic Church 525 (Christmas mystery).

■ **Parent's book** Just as Moses the shepherd saw the GLORY of the Lord on the mountain, so the shepherds of Bethlehem saw the GLORY on the hills of Bethlehem. Just like Moses, they were afraid, and yet once again there is a message of deliverance from God. Shepherds were "outside the law" as far as certain respectable people were concerned. They were unable to keep the strict laws of washing which the Pharisees followed and so were imprisoned in a "sinful" condition. Once again, God approaches people caught up in slavery, and gives them the Good News of peace: God is with us – Emmanuel.

Page 52 Church

It is probably very difficult for most children to see anything GLORIOUS in the Eucharist. Acknowledge their admission of boredom, if they say it. On the other hand, some children may have had a sense of awe sometimes – perhaps when the church was empty, or at a Mass with incense and candles. Perhaps they really enjoy singing certain hymns. They may like to sing a "Gloria" they have learnt at school.

References: Mass: Gloria, Sanctus; Catechism of the Catholic Church 1381 (not by the senses).

■ **Parent's book** The whole of the Eucharist is a prayer of praise and thanks to the **GLORY** of God. (The word "**Eucharist**" means "**thanksgiving**". In Greece today you can still hear people saying "**efhiristo**" – "**thank you**".)

At the Eucharist the children could listen out for how many times the word **GLORY** and similar words are mentioned. In their session they will be thinking about the **GLORIA**, but there are other important prayers of praise. The words of the Preface change, according to what aspect of God's glory we are praising and being thankful for. There is also the beautiful prayer:

Through him, and with him, and in him,
O God, almighty Father,
in the unity of the Holy Spirit,
all glory and honour is yours,
for ever and ever.

The response of **AMEN** is everyone's chance to make the prayer their own. The sound should raise the roof! The children could be encouraged to really shout it out!

When the shepherds left the magnificent glory of God on the hillside, they arrived at the quiet glory of a baby in a manger. At the Eucharist we meet the quiet glory of God in the consecrated bread and wine. The more we are aware of the wonder of the **REAL PRESENCE,** the more will our children appreciate this breathtaking **MYSTERY OF FAITH**.

Page 53

■ **Parent's book** Your child may like to do this page with another family member, a parent or a carer.

Page 54 *Family Time*

■ **Parent's book** Choose a place where you can talk about this page with your child and any other family member.

Look in a Mass book and find the words at the end of the Eucharistic Prayer. Do they match the words on this page?

Say the family prayer together, taking turns with each line.

Colour the flame of the little candle on this page.

PARENTS' SESSION

Adapt as you think appropriate.

As parents arrive, hand each a sheet with the following questions:

- **What takes you out of yourself?**

- **Have you ever been aware of the GLORIOUS presence of God?**

- **How can we encourage a sense of awe and wonder in our children?**

- **How can we make the Eucharist GLORIOUS for us and the children?**

- Tea/coffee/refreshments in groups.

- Short introduction welcoming parents, reminding them this session is about "GLORY" and giving them five minutes to look at "glorious" pictures scattered on tables, such as the baptism and transfiguration of Jesus.

- Parents then choose a picture to take back to the group.

- Go through questions on the sheet. Remember, all contributions are valid.

- Someone to read out loud to the whole group Luke's story of the shepherds.

- Another possibility to do in groups is to go through the words of the Mass and see how many times "GLORY" and associated words are used.

SERVICE *Glory to God in the highest*

You will need:
- **The cast: shepherds, angel**
- **Bulbs or corms**

Opening Prayer
Heavenly Father, we have been thinking about all the glorious things
you have given us. Help us to think more about your glory
as we listen to the Good News of the birth of Jesus.
We ask this through Jesus Christ, our Lord.
Amen.
Children to come forward and act out the story as it is read out to them.

Gospel: Luke 2:8-20
The shepherds.

Reflection
On glory. Draw responses about glorious times from children.

Prayers of Thanksgiving read by Children
(practised during session)
We thank you for the sudden glory of a rainbow.
We thank you for the quiet glory of the stars.
We thank you for the magnificent glory of fireworks.
We thank you for the wonderful glory of Jesus being born.
Children come up in pairs for a bulb.
Catechist: Plant this bulb and wait for the hidden glory to appear.
Child: Thank you.

Prayer
We thank you for the glory of the world, and the glory of our lives.
We thank you for the quiet glory of the stars, the sudden glory
of a rainbow, the magnificent glory of fireworks. We thank you
especially for your glorious love, which you showed by sending
Jesus to be our Saviour. *(Children go back to their places).*
All say Glory be to the Father…

NOTES

CHAPTER 6   THE WORD OF THE LORD
LITURGY OF THE WORD

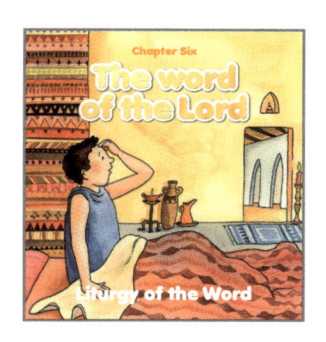

You will need:

- **A Bible or Missal (or Missalette) would be useful for the church section**
- **Dice and counters**

■ **Parent's book** In this session the children will be thinking about **LISTENING** to the word of God. The first part of the Eucharist includes what is called the Liturgy of the Word, and what we **LISTEN** to focuses our minds on a particular reason for glorifying God, depending on the season of the Church's year, the feast and the like.

Page 57 Everyday Life

Remember some children may have hearing problems. Be sensitive. Use experiences of grommets or hearing aids to stress how important it is to receive messages.

Reference: John 1:1-14 (In the beginning was the Word… and dwelt among us).

■ **Parent's book** The children have a "fun" start this session, thinking about how animals would survive without ears! They will then think about how well they themselves would survive if they didn't **LISTEN**. (The catechists are aware that some children may have hearing problems, and will be sensitive to this.) The idea is to help them consider how listening to the word of the Lord helps us to live in confidence as children of God.

Pages 58, 59 and 60 The Old Testament

Samuel is a foreshadowing of Jesus. Samuel, Jesus and the children are all linked. They are all special: children of God, consecrated to God, God knows them all by name, they can listen to God and have messages from God. For example: good ideas which suddenly come to them.

Reference: 1 Samuel 3:1-10 (the boy Samuel listens).

■ **Parent's book** The children read the story of Samuel in the Temple. Hannah had wept and prayed for a child, and promised him to the Lord if she should have one. When Samuel was born, Hannah sang a song of praise to God, recounting the marvellous saving works of God in lifting up the poor and feeding the hungry. Years later, Mary would use this song as a basis for her song of praise to God, when her cousin Elizabeth acknowledged the presence of the Saviour in Mary's womb. This prayer, known as the **Magnificat**, is still used every evening in the **Prayer of the Church** (Divine Office).

The children will concentrate on the story of Samuel hearing God call him in the night. The children are like Samuel in that they are gifts from God. Baptism not only marks their entry into the community, but also makes them "**prophets**" who hear God's word and carry it out to others, just as Samuel did. Holy Communion will mark their entry into full membership of the community and, as well as making them holy, will give them strength to be prophets: pro-God and pro-others.

Page 61 *The New Testament*

This links up with the quiet glory of the previous session. You have to have a deeper look at things to see the presence of God in them. There is nothing more wonderful than God becoming human. But a homeless family in a dirty stable? Oh dear! You have to look deeper!

References: Luke 2:15 (Let us go... and see this thing that has happened), Matthew 1:25.

■ **Parent's book** In the Old Testament, there were many prophets who brought God's word to the people. Jesus is more than the greatest of the prophets – he **IS** God's Word. Jesus is the embodiment of God. God responds to our poverty and need by becoming poor and needy. God is indeed **Emmanuel** – "**God with us**".

The word "**Bethlehem**" means "**House of Bread**". In Jesus, the songs of Hannah and Mary are fulfilled, for in him God comes to our rescue – the poor and hungry are fed.

The promise is kept today in the Eucharist when God is with us as the bread of life, and we go out from the Eucharist with a mission to feed the hungry – to be Christ's saving presence to those in need.

Page 62 *Picture to colour in*

Talk the children through the illustration as a revision of the previous chapter. God has an idea (very humanly speaking) and God's idea (word) is so powerful it is immediately effective. God's wish to save us is embodied in Jesus.

Page 63 Church

On this page the children are concentrating on Christ's presence at Mass in the readings. Show a Bible or Missal if you have one. You could practise saying the responses, and talk about standing for the Gospel as a mark of respect. (Jews and Orthodox Christians stand when praying, whereas we are inclined to kneel.)

For their picture, it doesn't matter what the setting is. It is important for them not to think that holy things only happen in church, but to realise that everyday life can also be holy. It is the things that happen in everyday life that we bring to the Eucharist each week. The readings, in turn, can help us to make sense of everyday life.

References: John 1:14 (the Word was made flesh), Catechism of the Catholic Church 1100-1102 (liturgy – word of God), Catechism of the Catholic Church 1153-1155 (word/action inseparable).

■ **Parent's book** The readings at the Eucharist are often above the heads of the children and they can get bored. If your parish has a special Liturgy of the Word for children, they listen and think about the readings at their own level of understanding. The responses for this part of the Mass could be practised with other family members, playing different roles.

Pages 64 to 65 Everyday Life

A listening-themed game for all to play.

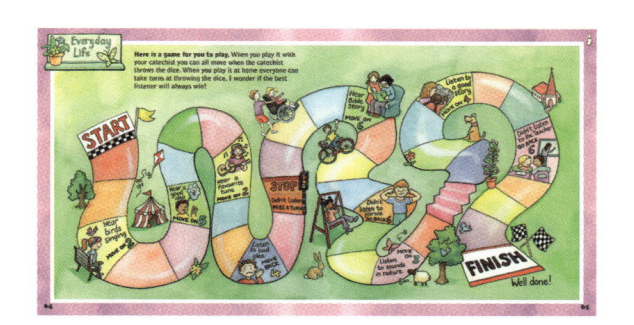

Page 66 Family Time

■ **Parent's book** Choose a place where you can talk about this page with your child and any other family member. Search the church together for the lectern and look for the Creed in a Mass book.

Perhaps light a candle and say the prayer together.

Encourage your child to use his or her book. Colour the flame of the candle in the top right-hand corner of each page that has one as you go through the book.

PARENTS' SESSION

- **Tea in groups.**

- **Short introduction welcoming parents, saying what children will be doing.**

- **LISTEN to a beautiful piece of music.**

- **Then... parents to say how the music affected them...**

- **Then:**

    What news would make you feel good this week?

    What are the obstacles to LISTENING?

    What message do you HEAR from the Church?

    How does it make you feel?

    How does it affect the way you live?

- **To think about...**

What messages do your children HEAR from you (about themselves, the Church, life)?

- **Finish with prayer (or similar) about listening.**

SERVICE   *The word of the Lord*

> **You will need:**
> - **The cast: Samuel, Eli, voice of God**
> - **Candles**
> - **Book of Gospels**
> - **Scrolls with individual messages on them**

Hymn
Here I am – *Verses 1 and 2*
Procession of the Book of Gospels (2 children with lights, 1 with Book of Gospels)

Opening Prayer
Heavenly Father, today we have been thinking about listening,
and how important it is.
Help us to listen carefully to the story of Samuel, as some of us act it out.
We ask this through Jesus Christ, our Lord.
Amen.
*Children to come forward and act out the story as it is read out to them
(Samuel, Eli, voice of God).*

Reading: 1 Samuel 3:1-10
Call of Samuel.

Reflection
About listening (favourite sounds/listening at Mass).
Children come up for scroll with a message from God on it.
Catechist: Receive the word of the Lord.
Child: Thank you.

Prayer
Father in heaven,
we thank you for all the wonderful sounds we hear.
We thank you for the sound of splashing water, for the sound of birds singing,
for the sound of friendly words we hear at home and at school.
We thank you especially for listening to us when we talk to you,
and for sending us Jesus, as your answer to our prayers.
Amen.

Hymn
Here I am – *Verse 3*

NOTES

CHAPTER 7 BREAD TO OFFER
LITURGY OF THE EUCHARIST

■ **Parent's book** Until now the children were thinking about the first part of the Eucharist – the **Liturgy of the Word**. They are now turning to the second part – the **Liturgy of the Eucharist**. In this session the children will be thinking about the Preparation of the Offerings/Offertory.

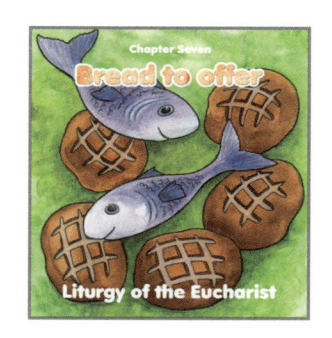

Pages 68 to 69 *Everyday Life*

Children can supply words for the pictures. Hopefully this is straightforward. During the discussion, once again be aware that some children may not live with their mother/father. Try to draw out from the children the following two opposite ideas. Food doesn't appear from nowhere, it is worked for. A good meal is the result of cooperation from everyone. Food is a real gift/blessing. Parents provide food for their children, even though children do little to earn it. The same is true in nature – very soon the birds will be devoting all their energies to building nests and feeding their young.

Reference: Gaudium et spes 34 (work of human hands).

■ **Parent's book** You will have more time than the catechists to discuss with your child all that has to happen before a meal can take place. You could think about some of the products you eat, the danger of deep sea fishing, the length of time the farmer has to care for the crop, and so on. Perhaps you could work out how many hours' work the food on your table costs!

Pages 70 to 71 *The Old Testament*

The children may like to retell what they remember about Moses. The time spent in the desert wasn't wasted time – the Israelites started out as a disorganised rabble of escaped slaves, but were gradually formed into a community. The story of the manna is the story of how God provides for God's children. Not only had they NOT worked for it, but they had grumbled about how hard life was, and wished they were back in slavery!

Reference: Exodus 16.

■ **Parent's book** The people in the desert were entirely at the mercy of God (and the heat, lack of food and water). In their wanderings they learnt to trust that God would provide, and developed a real understanding of what "**bread**" stands for. To a large extent we have lost this understanding, and maybe even lost a realisation of how dependent we are on God. When hardships hit us we can either grumble, like the Israelites did at first, or develop an attitude of trust in God, who "**gives us our daily bread**".

The Israelites were instructed to gather only enough for their daily needs. If they gathered too much, the manna putrefied. However, on the day before the Sabbath they were instructed to gather twice as much so they could rest on the Sabbath. This amount did not putrefy and they were able to eat on the day of rest. Throughout their journey the Israelites were fed on the manna, rather like we, the new people of God, are fed on the bread of life throughout our life's journey (see Exodus 16).

Pages 71 and 72 *The New Testament*

Moses was a saviour for his people, but Jesus is Saviour of the world. It would be worthwhile reading all of John 6 as a preparation for the parents' sessions, to see the context of the feeding of the five thousand. The words of Jesus after this miracle (sign) are all about the Eucharist: "I am the bread of life. Your fathers ate the manna in the desert, and they are dead... Anyone who eats this bread will live for ever, and the bread that I shall give is my flesh..." (John 6:48-51).

With the children, talk about the offering of the young boy.

Jesus took his meagre offering and turned it into something stupendous. This is what happens at the Eucharist – we offer bread, wine, money, our little sacrifices and triumphs of the week, and they are transformed into something wonderful.

Reference: John 6:1-13.

■ **Parent's book** Three of the Gospels, Matthew, Mark and Luke, give accounts of the Last Supper of Jesus. John does not. Instead, he puts his teaching about the Eucharist in chapter 6, the feeding of the five thousand. The children will be thinking about the little boy who offered up his five loaves and two fish. Jesus took these and enabled his disciples to feed the crowd with twelve baskets of scraps left over. As adults, we can go deeper into the mystery, and read all that Jesus said about himself after this great **sign**. One thing worth mentioning is that Jesus said, "**I am the bread of life**." He makes seven "**I AM**" statements in John's Gospel. You may remember that when Moses asked God's name he was told, "**I AM WHO I AM**." Jesus is telling us that he, God, the great I AM, is feeding us with his own self, and we shall live for ever.

Pages 74 to 75 *Church*

Stress the link with their own mealtimes. The words used for the ritual meal have everyday counterparts. Children of this age don't really understand symbols too well, they still take everything very literally, but they could discuss how the bread, wine and money stand for so much more. Also, encourage the children to take a more active part in the Eucharist. The more involved they are, the less bored they will be. A children's liturgy in your parish would also help them participate more fully.

References: Jewish Passover-style prayer at Mass – "work of human hands", Our Father: "...our daily bread".

44

■ **Parent's book** As said earlier, we are probably out of touch with the deep significance of presenting bread to God. We are so dependent on food that we are offering God our very existence. To put it less grandly, when we offer up the bread it stands for all the sweat and labour, the tedium of the past week – everything we do to keep a roof above our heads and the wolf from the door. The offering of the money is also deeply significant. It is not an interruption of the Eucharist, but very much part of it. At the beginning of the Bible, in Genesis 14, Melchizedek, the king of Salem and priest of God the Most High, offered bread and wine to God, and Abram (later called Abraham) gave him a tenth of all his wealth.

We will think about the wine next time.

Page 76 Everyday Life

Linking everyday meals with the Eucharist should help the children appreciate the value of meals at home and this in turn should help them understand the Eucharist more. Eucharist means thanksgiving. We turn to God (and parents) with grateful hearts for all we receive, and our gratitude prompts us to generosity in our turn. The two things we could do for those less fortunate than ourselves are to pray for them at the Eucharist and anywhere else we may be, and give up some of our pocket money for them. This is a good suggestion for Lent.

References: Catechism of the Catholic Church 2427 (work – meaning and value), The Common Good, CBCEW (London: 1996) 90 (work/cooperation with God).

■ **Parent's book** Just as the disciples fed the crowds with the bread, we go out to others to **feed the world.** Our gratitude to God opens up a spirit of generosity in us, and the Eucharist not only feeds us but empowers us to go out to others.

Page 78 Family time

■ **Parent's book** Choose a place where you can talk about this page with your child and any other family member.

Pray together the prayer or use one of your own; then bake bread together. You may like to say a grace before you begin your next meal; children may be familiar with a grace they say at school.

Certificate to go with the service on page 48. The template can be found at the back of the book.

God blesses the work I am doing for my

FIRST
HOLY COMMUNION

~

Blessed be God for ever

PARENTS' SESSION

- **Let parents know about what children are doing.**

- **Parents to discuss which phrases of the hymn, "In bread we bring you, Lord", have special meaning for them.**

- **Parents to do pie chart of time spent on "work of their hands" for their children.**

- **Presentation of how work becomes their offering.**

SERVICE   *Bread to offer*

You will need:
- **The children's books**
- **Certificate of Achievement**
- **Food, torches, blankets**

Children to present books to priest, processing from back of church.
Go to places as they will on Communion day.

Opening Prayer

Heavenly Father, every day you look after us with your unending love.
You send the sun and send the rain so that we can have our daily bread.
Help us to care for the beautiful world you give us so that no one may ever go hungry again.
Amen.

Modern Parable: Share

Once there was a group of friends. Matthew had a tent for his birthday, and they decided to play camping in one of their gardens. They each had warm clothes, and a torch for the night, and a picnic for their evening meal.

They had great fun all day, playing games and all sorts of interesting things.

When evening came they were very, very hungry. Matthew thought no one else had any food, so he kept his hidden. He thought he would eat it when everyone was asleep. Samantha knew she only had enough for herself, so she kept her food hidden as well. All the children kept the food hidden away, in case they had to share it. It got darker and darker, and the children got hungrier and hungrier. At last, Robert couldn't stand it any longer. He went into the tent and brought out his crisps and orange drink. Laura laughed and she went into the tent. She brought out some sandwiches. All the children began to laugh. They rushed away and brought out all sorts of goodies: sausage rolls, peanuts, jam tarts and much, much more.

They sat down in a circle and had the best picnic they had ever had in their lives.

Priest or catechist to talk about how the children's generosity changed what they had. Link this with the Mass; we give to God, God transforms it.
Children come up and receive their books back, with "certificate" inserted into "pocket".
Catechist: God bless the work you have done.
Child: Blessed be God for ever.

Closing Prayer
Our Father

Final Hymn
In bread we bring you, Lord

CHAPTER 8   FRUIT OF THE VINE

References: New covenant – Jeremiah 31:31 and Luke 22:20.

■ **Parent's book** In this session the children will be thinking about wine as we use it at the Eucharist, and why we use it. As adults we can understand that wine not only symbolises celebration, but also stands for sorrow – we talk of a cup of sorrow. If we share a cup with someone, we are intimately connected with them. We share their destiny. Although the children will touch on the sorrowful aspect, they will be concentrating on the joy of celebration.

Pages 81 to 82 Everyday life

Remember to be sensitive to the fact that some children may have experiences of alcoholism among their relations, and therefore have negative feelings about wine.
Reference: 1 Corinthians 13:11 (when I was a child...).

■ **Parent's book** Often children don't like the taste of wine, so on their first page they will be thinking about tastes they didn't like when they were younger, but do like now. This links in with the idea of **sacrifice** and wine. They had to give up the comfort of a bottle in order to appreciate other drinks/food. Hopefully it will also prepare them for the practicalities of drinking the Blood of Christ at their First Eucharist. At home you might like them to taste wine if they haven't yet done so. Communion wine is usually sweet and rich.

Pages 83 to 84 The Old Testament

Over three thousand years ago, the Jewish people were enslaved by the Egyptians. God told Moses that a terrible event was about to overwelm Egypt, but that the Jews would be spared if they put lamb's blood on their doorways. Seeing the blood, God would "pass over" the house and the occupants would be safe. This was the first "Passover" (see Exodus 12). Make the link between the Passover lamb and the Lamb of God. To the Jews blood was synonymous with LIFE, and when talking about the Blood of Christ in the chalice, emphasise receiving Christ, or the life of Christ. When talking about Isaiah's song you could say Isaiah was a PROPHET, whose job it was to call people back to the covenant when they went astray. To make the point about sour grapes and sweet grapes you could give the children something sour (grapes or grapefruit?) and then something sweet (sweet grapes?). You may be able to incorporate sweet/sour-tasting foods into the service for this session.
References: Isaiah 5:1-2 (sour grapes), Isaiah 27:2-6 (the Lord's vineyard), Psalm 80 (vineyard out of Egypt), Hosea 2:14-17 (God's love for Israel), Catechism of the Catholic Church 1096 (Jewish/Christian liturgy).

■ **Parent's book** The Passover feast is held every spring to celebrate the deliverance of the people of God from slavery. The feast was not just held in memory of the past. To the Jews, celebrating this feast makes God's saving action present and available to them in the here and now.

The people of God thought of themselves as the vineyard of God. Other references to themselves as God's vineyard are in Psalm 80: **"There was a vine: you uprooted it from Egypt… Lord of Hosts, relent! Look down from heaven… look at this vine, visit it, protect what your own right hand has planted."**

Pages 85 to 86 The New Testament

John doesn't talk about miracles – he calls them "signs". His Gospel is sometimes called the *Book of Signs*. This incident at a marrige feast at Cana is the first sign of who Jesus is. The children may have been to weddings themselves. Stress the celebration aspect. Jesus is Good News. This story is NOT about children obeying their mothers, no matter how tempting it is to do a bit of moralising!

References: John 2:1-12 (miracle at Cana), Luke 22:17-18 (new wine in kingdom), Revelation 19:7 (wedding feast of the Lamb).

■ **Parent's book** The children will think about the celebration that Jesus provided at the wedding feast at Cana. So many gallons of wine is really lavish – rather like the miracle of the loaves and fishes when twelve baskets were left over! The abundance of wine is a symbol that the fullness of the kingdom has arrived (Isaiah 25:6). As adults, we can read more into the miracle (sign). It was "on the third day" which links with the resurrection. Jesus took the water (standing for the observances attached to the Sinai covenant?) and changed it into wine (standing for the observances of the new covenant?).

Pages 88 to 90 Church

There is a lot of text on page 88. It might be better for you to read it rather than the children. You could divide it into three parts (past, present and future) and stop for discussion after each part.

(a) **Past.** Make the link between the Passover prayer (page 83 of the children's book) and the prayer in the Eucharist, "Blessed are you, Lord God of all creation…"

At the Eucharist the children can also think about the recent past – all that has happened in the last week. They can offer thanks for the good things, and offer up any hardships they have suffered.

(b) **Present**. They could think of how being together at the Eucharist strengthens their friendship with one another and above all with Christ. They could also think of ways that the Eucharist IS a celebration. (Similarities to a party = flowers, candles, songs, special clothes, gifts.)

(c) **Future.** The Eucharist is a pledge of future happiness in heaven, and it brings about this union with God here and now. In gratitude for all we receive from God we remember at the Eucharist those less fortunate than ourselves. We also go out to these people in order to help bring about the time promised in scripture, when God lives among us. The term NEW COVENANT is only mentioned once in the Old Testament in Jeremiah 31 when God promises a new time when the law is written in people's hearts, and God and the people dwell together. This term is used several times in the New Testament, including by Christ at the Last Supper. You could remind the children of the meaning of the word Emmanuel – God with us.

References: John 15:5-10 (vine and branches), 1 Corinthians 10:16 (the cup of blessing), Mark 14:25 (new wine in kingdom), Catechism of the Catholic Church 1334 (wine – eschatological), Catechism of the Catholic Church 1340 (future Passover).

■ **Parent's book** The link between the Jewish Passover and the Eucharist is very obvious in the Passover prayer (on page 83 in the children's book). The Eucharist is very much a thank you prayer for all the good things of creation.

We also think of ourselves as a vine. Jesus said he was the vine and we are the branches. He is not separate from us: a vine IS the branches – we are the new risen body of Christ. "**In so far as you did it to one of the least of these brothers of mine, you did it to me**," says Jesus.

Just as the Passover makes God's saving action present to the Jews, so the Eucharist makes God's saving action present to us. We are liberated from slavery and sin by receiving the life of Christ. We look not only to the past, to Christ's redeeming acts of death and resurrection, but also to the future. At the Last Supper Jesus said he would not drink wine again until he drank the new wine of the kingdom of his Father. At the Eucharist God brings about the wedding feast of the Lamb, and eats with ever-growing people of God.

Page 89 *Everyday Life*

This page talks about the sacrificial aspect of the Eucharist. Explain the "Blood of Christ" as about receiving Christ, or the life of Christ, or the cup of salvation. Christ is received whole and entire under the appearance of bread or of wine.

On this page you could develop the sacrificial aspect of the Eucharist, and Christ's giving his life for us, and link it with all the ways the adults they live with give their lives for them.

Encourage them to see that if they put up with hardship for the sake of others they are being Christ-like, and are assisting God in bringing about a better world.

References: Matthew 20:22 (can we drink the cup of suffering?), Romans 8:17 (we share in his sufferings/glory), Revelation 21:1-4 (new earth), Catechism of the Catholic Church 793 (Christ unites us with his Passover), Lumen gentium 48 (new heaven and earth).

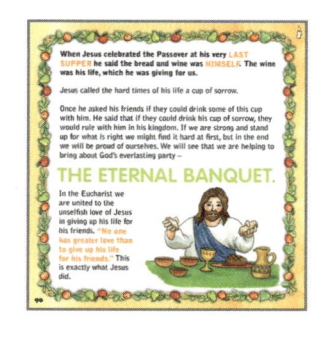

■ **Parent's book** The coming of the kingdom of God means that we must take the Eucharist seriously. Properly understood, the Eucharist means that we join with Jesus in bringing the Good News of the kingdom to the world no matter what the cost.

In the Eucharist we are uniting ourselves to the selfless love of Jesus who gave up his life for the world: "**God loved the world so much that he gave his only Son**" (John 3:16). Jesus calls his disciples "friends" and tells them: "**A man can have no greater love than to lay down his life for his friends**" (John 15:13).

Page 92 *Family Time*

■ **Parent's book** Choose a place where you can talk about this page with your child and any other family member.

This is a shared activity: cut and paste pictures while you discuss the happy and sad state of our world.

Perhaps light a candle and say the prayer together.

SERVICE *Fruit of the Vine*

You will need:
- **The cast: bride, groom, Jesus, Mary, guests (ten or more children)**
- **Wine gums, food for wedding feast, glass tumbler, cochineal (previously placed in bottom of tumbler), glass jug of water**

Opening Prayer

Heavenly Father, you give us all the good things of life. You give us food to give us strength, and drink to refresh us. When we eat together and drink together we grow closer to one another and to you. Blessed are you, Lord God of all creation.
Amen.

Children to come up and act out the marriage feast of Cana.
Water changed into wine.

Gospel: John 2:1-12

Reflection

Priest or catechist to talk about the importance of drink at a party.
A meal not complete without drink.
At Cana they thought it was water but it was wine.
At the Eucharist it looks like wine but it is Jesus.
(Talk about consecration).
Children come up and receive wine gums.
Catechist: Take these wine gums and enjoy them.
Child: Thank you.

Prayer

Father, we thank you for caring for us all. We thank you for our daily food and drink which give us strength for the hard times of life, and which help us enjoy the good times. We thank you especially for Jesus, who is soon to become our spiritual food and drink, when we receive him in the Holy Eucharist. Help us to prepare for this special meal which we are going to receive for the first time in just a few weeks' time. We ask this through Christ our Lord.
Amen.

Hymn

Give me joy in my heart

NOTES

CHAPTER 9   DO THIS IN MEMORY OF ME

In this session the children will be practising with bread and wine in the church.

- **Parent's book** We now come to the heart of the Eucharistic Prayer, the "**institution narrative**". At this part of the Eucharist the Holy Spirit is invoked: "Make holy, therefore, these gifts, we pray, by sending down your Spirit upon them…", and the **words of consecration** are said. Jesus is made present on the altar in a new way. His presence remains in the consecrated hosts reserved in the tabernacle in the sanctuary. The word "tabernacle" means "tent", specifically the tent of meeting in the desert (Exodus 25:8). Jesus is already present, in scripture, in the priest and people, and in other ways, but this new presence is so special it is called the **real presence**. In this sacrament Jesus is present in a unique way, whole and entire, fully God and fully human, substantially and permanently.

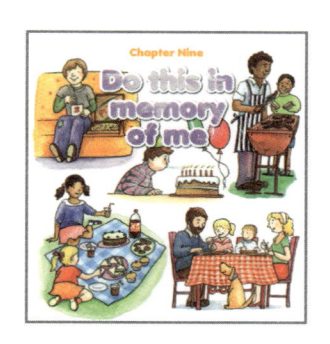

Pages 94 to 95 *Everyday Life*

The jumbled words are: picnics, barbecues, takeaways, parties, family meals. Meals can be occasions when we get to know one another… make up… celebrate someone… celebrate an event… relax…

- **Parent's book** We have meals for all sorts of reasons – for comfort, because we are hungry, to sustain us, to celebrate, to sit down and relax. Meals can be quick snacks in railway cafes, where we pay more attention to our luggage than the food and company, a great banquet in honour of someone special, an impromptu barbecue when friends call or a relaxing gathering of the family.

    Some meals really change us in some way. Sharing the same food and conversation can bring us closer together, and we gain new insights into each other and into the topics of conversation.

Page 96 *The Old Testament*

Be careful not to talk too much about sacrificing lambs. Some children are upset when they realise that the roast they have on Sunday was once a cute bird/animal. This section is here to stress the connection between the Passover, the Last Supper, the Eucharist (and Calvary). If you have time, you could give the children some unleavened bread or matzos and some blackcurrant juice, and have a little Passover-style feast.

References: Exodus 12:8-11 (unleavened bread/meal eaten in haste), Exodus 12:14-17 (keep feast as a memorial), Catechism of the Catholic Church 1334 (unleavened bread/haste).

■ **Parent's book** There is only one page on the Old Testament in this chapter. This is because we are concentrating more on the Last Supper, and we have talked about the Passover before. However, it might be worth noting that the word "Passover" comes from the fact that the Israelites sacrificed a lamb, and put the blood on their doorposts so that God "**passed over**" their houses. Because of the blood of the lamb, the Israelites did not suffer the tenth plague – the death of the eldest son.

Pages 97 to 98 The New Testament

You could discuss how the children would feel if a friend "betrayed" them. Probably very angry and vindictive! Jesus was still full of love on the night he was betrayed. See parent's book for more details.

References: Eucharistic Prayer III (night he was betrayed), Luke 22:19 (do this in memory of me), 1 Corinthians 11:23-25 (do in memory of me).

■ **Parent's book** Jesus took an existing feast, the most important of the Jewish celebrations, and changed it into something new. Throughout the Old Testament, God is constantly renewing the covenant made with human beings. In the book of Jeremiah, God promises a new covenant, not like the previous one. In the new covenant, "**Deep within them I will plant my Law, writing it on their hearts. Then I will be their God and they shall be my people... they will all now know me, the least no less then the greatest... I will forgive their iniquity and never call their sin to mind**" (Jeremiah 31:31-34).

Jesus brought about this new covenant at his Last Supper when he, the new Lamb of God, offered his life, present in the bread and in the cup of salvation (the blood of the new and everlasting covenant).

Page 99 Picture to colour in

Note that there is a gap in the picture to draw the child into the scene of Jesus with his friends at the Last Supper.

Pages 100 to 101 Church

The main thing to stress is that the whole point of the Eucharist is LOVE. John says "God is love", and the Incarnation is the perfect sacrament (sign) of the love of God. We receive this love in the Eucharist.

The Father is love – Jesus the Son is love – we receive love – we become love. A major theme of this session is CHANGE. The obvious change is the bread and wine, but we change too. Just as our everyday diet affects our health, our behaviour, who we are, so this spiritual food affects our spiritual life, behaviour, identity.

References: Catechism of the Catholic Church 1362-1366 (Eucharist = memorial sacrifice, past made present), Catechism of the Catholic Church 1103 (anamnesis).

■ **Parent's book** At the Eucharist, help your child to listen out for the words of consecration and the Lamb of God. If your child asks **HOW** Christ is present, perhaps tell them that Jesus said it would be so and Jesus always keeps his promises. Then perhaps prime him or her in readiness for the next session when we will look at how, after the resurrection, Jesus' body was so transformed he could pass through locked doors and his friends didn't recognise him! The mystery of Christ present in the Eucharist is so amazing it is called **THE MYSTERY OF FAITH.**

Page 102 Everyday Life

You could use this as a revision page. The children thought about baptism at their very first session. You could show them the links between the slaves of Egypt journeying in the desert and becoming a people, and how we would be slaves to sin if Jesus hadn't freed us. Our life is like the desert, in that we are on the way and we are fed and formed into a people by the Eucharist.

References: Catechism of the Catholic Church 1368 (our/Church's sacrifice), Catechism of the Catholic Church 1391-1398 (fruits of the Eucharist).

■ **Parent's book** Enjoy your meals together. Make them life-giving occasions!

Page 104 Family Time

■ **Parent's book** Choose a place where you can talk about this page with your child and any other family member.

Search the church for Our Lady's chapel, if there is one. Then talk about the Rosary.

Think about the words of Jesus: "**Do this in memory of me**."

The prayer to say invites one to "**customise**" it, according to who is sharing the prayer.

PARENTS' SESSION

- Tea and welcome.

- "Housekeeping" points.

- Parents to sit round a table with a treasured "souvenir" of their child. They can then talk about it (thus bringing it to life).

- Catechist input on the Passover meal Christ was celebrating.

- If you have a **DVD** of *Jesus of Nazareth* (Last Supper section) and one of last year's **First Communion**, these would be useful.

SERVICE   *Do this in memory of me*

You will need:
- **Cast: Jesus, apostles**
- **Table with bread**
- **Chalice, plate, cups**

Children to enter church as they will on their First Holy Communion day.

Opening Prayer

Father in heaven,
today we have been thinking about picnics and barbecues, takeaways and parties.
We have been thinking especially about the
Last Supper that Jesus had with his friends before he died.
Help us to understand more and more how much Jesus loves us,
and how wonderful it will be
to receive him into our hearts when we make
our First Holy Communion.
Amen.

Children to re-enact the Gospel of the Last Supper.

Gospel: Matthew 26:26-29

Reflection

Priest to talk about it.
Children come up and practise receiving bread and wine.

Catechist: This will become the bread of life.
Child: Amen.

Catechist: This will become the cup of salvation.
Child: Amen.

Prayer

Father in heaven, you give us Jesus to be the bread of life
and the cup of salvation. We thank you for your great love,
and we ask you to make us loving too,
through Christ our Lord.
Amen.

Hymn

Lord Jesus Christ

NOTES

CHAPTER 10   BODY OF CHRIST

Remember that we are not trying to "explain away" the Eucharist – it IS a mystery. Stress how marvellous it is. (A theological mystery is not like an Agatha Christie novel where we try to find out who did it. It is something so wonderful that no matter how much we know about it, there is always more to learn. It is an inexhaustible treasure.)

■ **Parent's book** In this session we are looking at the words the priest says as he distributes the host and the chalice – "**The Body of Christ**" and "**The Blood of Christ**". We are thinking about HOW Christ is present in the bread and wine.

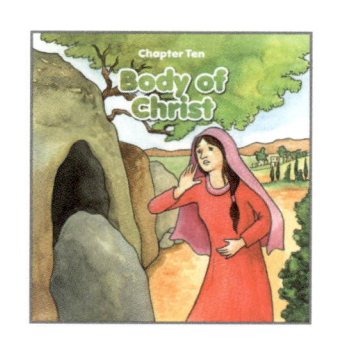

Page 106 Do you know?

Page 107 Everyday life

We are not trying to give a biology lesson, but trying to instil a sense of wonder in the children. Outward appearances can change, but the inner reality is the same.

■ **Parent's book** The children will be thinking about how tadpoles and caterpillars change into frogs and butterflies. The outer appearances change, but the inner reality is the same. They will be led to think about how the opposite happens at the Eucharist. At Mass the outer appearances of the bread and wine are the same, but the inner reality is different.

In order to have two New Testament stories, there is no Old Testament story in this chapter. The Old Testament stories have been leading up to the fulfilment of God's promise in the new covenant.

61

Pages 109, 110 and 112 *The New Testament*

These pages lead on from page 107 (outwardly different but inwardly the same). This is what Jesus was like after the resurrection. His closest friends didn't recognise him. You might like to look up other resurrection stories to show that Christ was the same yet different after the resurrection. "Thomas" is a good one (this story also says "Blessed are those who have not seen and yet believe". You could point out that this means US). Jesus seems to have a habit of disappearing as soon as he is recognised in the "breaking of bread".
References: John 20:11-18 (appearance to Mary Magdalene), Luke 24:13-35 (Emmaus).

■ **Parent's book** The two stories (Christ appearing to Mary Magdalene, and to the friends on the way to Emmaus) have been chosen to illustrate the fact that Jesus looked different. He had a different kind of body. At home you could remind your children of Christ's appearances in the upper room, first when Thomas was absent, then when he was there. Christ's body could go through locked doors, but he wasn't a ghost – he ate with them, and Thomas could touch him. After the resurrection Jesus could appear as a gardener, a stranger, he could come and go suddenly and mysteriously. He was not limited by the normal constraints of human life. And yet, it was the same Jesus whom they knew and loved. At Emmaus, the friends recognised him in the "**breaking of bread**" – in the Eucharist.

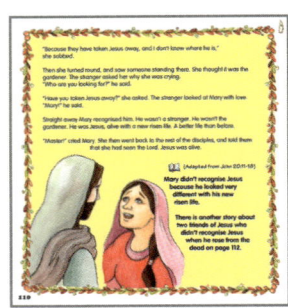

Page 113 *Church*

As a preparation for you as an adult it might be worth looking at 1 Corinthians 11:17-34, remembering that the term "body of Christ" can be used for both the Eucharist and the people of God. People in Corinth were eating and drinking the body and blood of Christ, while at the same time ignoring/humiliating the body of Christ – the people.

Page 113 concentrates on Christ present in the visible signs of bread and wine. What happens is different from our normal experience, for here the outward appearances remain the same, while the inner reality changes.
References: Sacrosanctum concilium 7 (modes of Christ's presence), Catechism of the Catholic Church 1105 (epiclesis), Catechism of the Catholic Church 1373-1377 (presence of Christ by word and Spirit, real presence, transubstantiation).

■ **Parent's book** It is in the Eucharist that we recognise Jesus too. We look at the outward appearances of bread and wine, but recognise Jesus in the "**breaking of bread**". It is such a unique mystery, so it is called the **MYSTERY OF FAITH**. The introduction about tadpoles and caterpillars is more about the wonder of the changes that they can see, to prepare them for the wonder of the change that they can't see.

62

Page 114 *Everyday Life*

You might have time to develop the idea that just as Christ still keeps his wounds as marks of love, so we are wounded people, the body of Christ. Their First Communion day won't be perfect in every way, but this is only to be expected. Life in the family, in the Church, and in the world can be quite messy, but at least Christ is in the middle of the mess, redeeming it by his presence. It is this presence of Christ in our midst that gives us hope, and makes us a thankful ("eucharistic") people.

References: John 6:56 (he who eats my flesh… I live in him), 1 Corinthians 12:12-30 (one body – many parts), Catechism of the Catholic Church 1391 (Communion augments our union with Christ), Catechism of the Catholic Church 1396 (Eucharist makes the Church).

■ **Parent's book** There is so much to say, and so little time! When we go to the Eucharist sometimes we feel wonderful, sometimes we feel hypocritical, sometimes we feel we have the strength to conquer the world afterwards, sometimes we go back to old bad habits. The truth of it is that we are a wounded people, just as Jesus was wounded. If we could try to look at one another in the community, and indeed in the world, and see this body of Christ, and love one another with the compassion of Christ, the Eucharist will have borne fruit. There will be more about this aspect of the Eucharist in the next session, but for this one, in the last week or so before your child's Communion, encourage him or her to pray quietly to Jesus. And pray together as a family if you feel you can do so. Bearing in mind that children may not feel anything very much after their First Holy Communion (there are a lot of practicalities for them to think about, and they might be nervous), tell them that the time after receiving the Eucharist is a very special time, both for them and Jesus. Time spent in stillness and reverence will help them to "**recognise him in the breaking of bread**".

*Once again the children will be practising with
the bread and wine in church towards the end of their session
instead of having a service.
Please stress that after Communion the children
should try to be still and "savour" the presence of Christ.
If they are fidgety and chatty they will lose out on a special moment.
Also, encourage them to smile during the service:
it is a happy occasion.*

Page 116 *Family Time*

■ **Parent's book** Choose a place where you can talk about this page with your child and any other family member. There may be many memories worth sharing with one another from grandparents through to siblings.
  Talk about your child's First Communion day and who will be sharing it, as it needs some organising. Just as important, write a prayer letter to Jesus and share it with the family's own prayers at prayer time.

NOTES

CHAPTER 11   TO LOVE AND TO SERVE
CONCLUDING RITES

You may find you are beginning to run out of time by this session but please make sure the children do the letter to their prayer sponsor if nothing else. Do that first.

■ **Parent's book** Our last session of the programme! This will be a shorter session than the earlier ones to allow time for a party at the end. Please encourage your child to finish his or her book at home. We will be concentrating on getting the children to write a "**thank you letter**" to their prayer sponsors. Some of you may have already asked your children to do this. Your child will also be given the name of a new child to pray for next year.

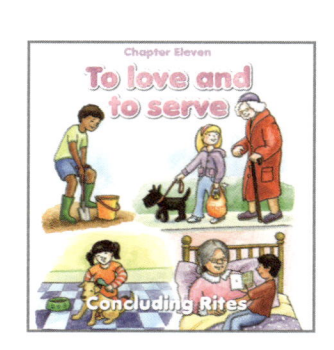

Pages 118 to 119 *Everyday Life*

This is to prepare the children for...
   (a) Communion gives us strength for life.
   (b) Others do not have enough to eat, to live, to grow, to be happy.

■ **Parent's book** At mealtimes you could make the link between everyday food and spiritual food. Communion gives us strength for living as Christians. If we don't eat of this food regularly we might grow weak spritually. The Eucharist is called the "**source and summit**" of the Christian life.

   If you don't normally thank God for your food at mealtimes, you might like to introduce this and add a prayer for those who haven't enough to eat.

Page 120 *The Old Testament*

Remind the children of the importance of names (Chapter 1).
   This entry into the Promised Land was the fulfilment of God's promise to Abraham. It represents the kingdom of God to us. When the Jews were faithful to the covenant they were always careful to care for the widow and orphan.

References: Joshua 3 (crossing the Jordan), Deuteronomy 8:7-10 (promise of fertile land), Deuteronomy 10:19 (protect the stranger, you were a stranger once).

■ **Parent's book** There won't be enough time to remind the children of the whole story of humanity as seen through the eyes of the Jewish people. You could go back over the whole of your child's work book (or, better still, a children's Bible) and trace the story from Adam and Eve to the entry into the Promised Land. When the people were in the Promised Land they had time to work out their laws, traditions, feasts and so on. In fact, it was only after they settled down that they wrote down the stories of Adam and Eve, Abraham and the others.

65

Pages 121 to 122 *The New Testament*

Another of the post-resurrection appearances. Once again Jesus is a stranger – just someone on the beach.

References: John 21:1-17 (lakeside appearance, feed my sheep), Matthew 25:34-40 (I was hungry…).

■ **Parent's book** This story, like the one of Emmaus last session, is a "**model**" of the Eucharist. Christ feeds us and asks us to do likewise: "**Feed my lambs and sheep.**" Note that the apostles, including trained fishermen, couldn't catch fish themselves. There are many other stories you could tell your children about how we help bring about the kingdom of God (how we enter the Promised Land). For example: "**I was hungry and you gave me food**" is a good one (Matthew 25:34-40).

Page 124 *Family Time*

■ **Parent's book** Choose a place where you can talk about this page with your child and any other family member.

Look at the prayers suggested to say together, and work out what they mean to different members of the family; your wider family; the family of the parish and the family of the school.

Pages 125 to 126 *Church*

The word "Mass" comes from the Latin "Missa" – to be sent. We go to Mass in order to be sent out. This links with the New Testament story where Jesus feeds his friends and tells them to feed others. The name reinforces the message.

References: Catechism of the Catholic Church 1394 (Eucharist strengthens our charity), Catechism of the Catholic Church 1397 (Eucharist commits us to the poor).

■ **Parent's book** Sometimes people say they don't need to go to church as they are just as good as churchgoers, or even that churchgoers are hypocrites. This may be true, as we are a church of sinners, but the Eucharist, properly understood, strengthens us to serve others. What we put into it and what we receive from it have a direct bearing on how we live every day.

Page 126 *Thank you*

Please make sure children do this page. You have a list of prayer sponsors so the children can fill in the name. Gather up the letters at the end of the session so that they can be sent to the sponsors with a photograph of the child, plus a request to pray for a child next year.

Reference: Eucharisticum mysterium, 13 (influence of Eucharist on daily life).

Allow time for a party for the children at the end of this session.

Thanks be to God!
We are a Eucharistic (thankful) people.

NOTES

Appendices

My Prayers

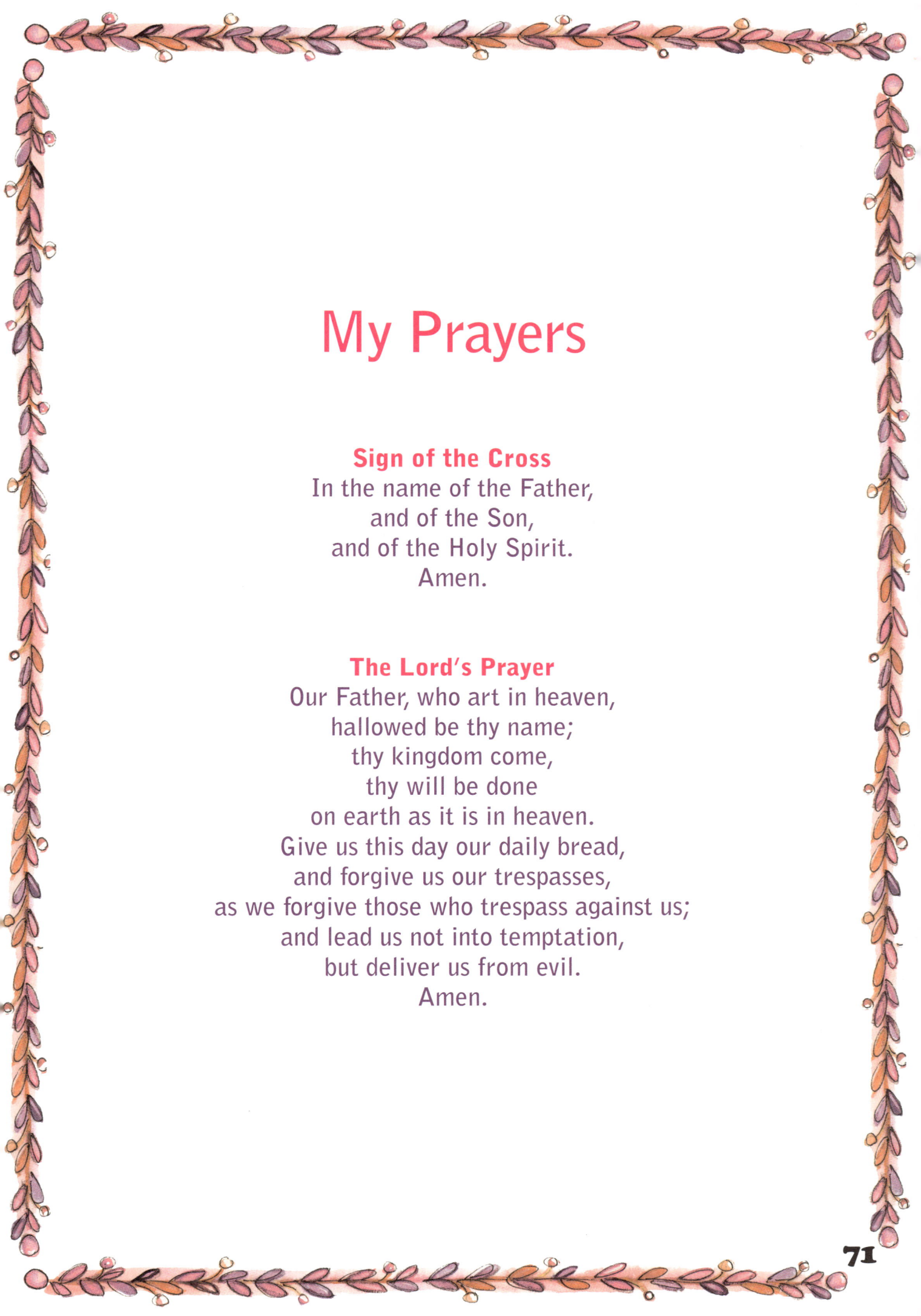

Sign of the Cross
In the name of the Father,
and of the Son,
and of the Holy Spirit.
Amen.

The Lord's Prayer
Our Father, who art in heaven,
hallowed be thy name;
thy kingdom come,
thy will be done
on earth as it is in heaven.
Give us this day our daily bread,
and forgive us our trespasses,
as we forgive those who trespass against us;
and lead us not into temptation,
but deliver us from evil.
Amen.

Hail Mary
Hail, Mary, full of grace,
the Lord is with thee.
Blessed art thou among women,
and blessed is the fruit
of thy womb, Jesus.
Holy Mary, Mother of God,
pray for us sinners,
now and at the hour of our death.
Amen.

Glory be to the Father
Glory be to the Father and to the Son and to the Holy Spirit,
as it was in the beginning, is now, and ever shall be,
world without end.
Amen.

Grace before Meals
Thank you, Lord, for this food
and for those who prepared it.
Bless us as we share your gifts.
Amen.

Prayer of Thanksgiving
Thank you, Lord, for all your gifts to me.
Help me to use them in your service.
Amen.

Renewal of Baptismal Promises

Let us renew the promises of Holy Baptism, by which we once renounced Satan and his works and promised to serve God in the holy Catholic Church. And so I ask you:

Priest: Do you renounce Satan?
People: I do.

Priest: And all his works?
People: I do.

Priest: And all his empty show?
People: I do.

Priest: Do you believe in God, the Father almighty, Creator of heaven and earth?
People: I do.

Priest: Do you believe in Jesus Christ, his only Son, our Lord, who was born of the Virgin Mary, suffered death and was buried, rose again from the dead and is seated at the right hand of the Father?
People: I do.

Priest: Do you believe in the Holy Spirit, the holy Catholic Church, the communion of saints, the forgiveness of sins, the resurrection of the body, and life everlasting?
People: I do.

And may almighty God, the Father of our Lord Jesus Christ, who has given us new birth by water and the Holy Spirit and bestowed on us forgiveness of our sins, keep us by his grace, in Christ Jesus our Lord, for eternal life.
Amen.

Eucharistic Responses

Penitential Act
Priest: …Lord, have mercy *or* Kyrie, eleison.
People: Lord, have mercy *or* Kyrie, eleison.
Priest: …Christ, have mercy *or* Christe, eleison
People: Christ, have mercy *or* Christe, eleison.
Priest: …Lord, have mercy *or* Kyrie, eleison.
People: Lord, have mercy *or* Kyrie, eleison.

Liturgy of the Word
After the first (and second) reading:
Reader: The word of the Lord.
People: Thanks be to God.
Before the Gospel:
Priest or deacon: The Lord be with you.
People: And with your spirit.
Priest or deacon: A reading from the holy Gospel according to…
People: Glory to you, O Lord.
After the reading of the Gospel:
Priest: The Gospel of the Lord.
People: Praise to you, Lord Jesus Christ.

Eucharistic Acclamation
Priest: The mystery of faith:
People: We proclaim your Death, O Lord, and profess your Resurrection until you come again.

or

People: When we eat this Bread and drink this Cup, we proclaim your Death, O Lord, until you come again.

or

People: Save us, Saviour of the world, for by your Cross and Resurrection you have set us free.

The Sign of Peace
Priest: The peace of the Lord be with you always.
People: And with your spirit.

The priest or deacon invites the people to give the sign of peace.

Priest or deacon: Let us offer each other the sign of peace.

At Mass we usually exchange a sign of peace by shaking hands with those around us.

Just before Communion
**All: Lord, I am not worthy
that you should enter under my roof,
but only say the word
and my soul shall be healed.**

Dismissal
Priest or deacon:
Go forth, the Mass is ended.

or

Go and announce the Gospel of the Lord.

or

Go in peace, glorifying the Lord by your life.

or

Go in peace.

People: Thanks be to God.

Special Words

Baptism: The sacrament through which I became a member of God's Christian family, the Church and through which I was cleansed of original sin.

Blessed Sacrament: The real presence of Jesus in the form of consecrated bread.

Body of Christ: A name for Holy Communion and also for the family of the Church.

Bread of life: A name for the sacrament of Jesus in Holy Communion.

Christian: Christian is the name given to followers of Christ.

Eucharist: Comes from a Greek word meaning "to give thanks". It is often used for the Mass and the Body and Blood of Jesus in particular.

Eucharistic Prayer: A prayer praising God; calling down the Holy Spirit; retelling the Last Supper story; and with the words of Jesus, changing the bread into his body and the wine into his blood.

Host: The bread that is used in the Mass after it becomes the body of the Lord Jesus.

Lamb of God: A name Christians give to Jesus.

Last Supper: The special meal which Jesus shared with his friends the night before he died.

Liturgy: The worship of God in public prayer. The liturgy of the Church is made up of ceremonies for which there are clear guidelines.

Mass: Also called the Eucharist – the celebration of the death and resurrection of Jesus.

Sacrifice: Means "to offer". During the Mass, the priest, in the name of the people, makes present again Christ's offering of himself to the Father. We recognise that Jesus is Lord and Saviour and that we believe in him.

NOTES

LETTER TO GRANDPARENTS

Dear Grandparent,

You are reading this because your grandchild is preparing for his or her First Holy Communion. You may be a silver-haired old grandad, a glamorous young granny, or somebody quite different. You may be a devout churchgoer, an atheist, or something in-between these two. But whoever or whatever you are, your grandchild is taking an important step in preparing for First Holy Communion, and your loving involvement can enrich the whole process.

Your grandchild's first steps

A child's first steps are very precious. You can probably remember when your own child was learning to walk, and if you were lucky you were there when your grandchild began to toddle. You had to decide how much help to give, and when to let go. There were many tumbles but, with some tears and much laughter, the infant began to walk. You may have had mixed feelings as your child grew from dependence to independence.

You may also have mixed feelings as your grandchild takes the step of preparing for First Holy Communion. It will depend on your relationship with the Catholic Church. You may be delighted, dubious or aghast at the idea! If your feelings are different from those of the child's parent(s) this could be a complication, and you will need to use the wisdom and diplomacy that come with maturity.

Freedom of choice

If your journey towards wholeness and fulfilment follows a different path from your grandchild, please remember that – with his or her parent(s) – he or she has decided to walk in full communion with the Catholic Church, and to be nourished in that journey by Jesus, the bread of life. No matter how painful this may be, please respect their freedom to choose, and take an interest in your grandchild's preparation. If you feel badly towards the Catholic Church, you may find that a closer look gives you a pleasant surprise.

Perhaps you are a fully committed Catholic, and have had to do a lot of running around to ensure that your grandchild is brought up as a Catholic because your own child does not go to church often. If you are reading this letter, you have probably succeeded in getting your grandchild enrolled in preparation sessions, but tact will be necessary here also. Just as you can't force a baby to walk before he or she is ready, so you can't force a child to love God in the way you do. You need the wisdom to know when to encourage and when to stand back. Pray for your grandchild and his or her family. Keep up to date with church teaching so that you can answer questions if necessary.

New insights

If you and your family attend church regularly, you are in a happy position. Not only can your faith be a shining example to everyone, you will probably find that your grandchild will give you new insights into the Eucharist. Children have an uncanny knack of asking very searching questions. You may find that as you search for answers, your relationship with Christ takes on a new lease of life you didn't think was possible.

The following thoughts may help you to understand more fully the important step your grandchild is taking, and how closely you are involved.

- Love cannot contain itself and one of the fruits of your love for your partner was your child. Just as Jesus said to those he loved at the Last Supper, you said to your partner, "This is my body, given for you." This giving was not a one-off thing, but a way of life. Now you can look back and see how, in the good times and the bad times, your body has been given and your life's blood has been poured out for those you love. Your giving of your life was, literally, life-giving.

- Your body may not be all that it once was! Like Jesus, you bear the marks of love, of daily sacrifice for your family. But like Jesus, you live to see the fruits of that love – the love that will not contain itself, but is reborn in your children and your children's children.

In the next few months your grandchild is going to reflect more and more on the life-giving love God gives us in Jesus, and which is shown most clearly in the Eucharist, the sacrament of love. Your grandchild will discover how he or she is part of the divine plan of love, and that by sharing in the Eucharist he or she is strengthened to love God, his or her family and the whole world. You and your grandchild are caught up in this mystery. Enjoy this time of preparation together, and enjoy the life-giving fruits of the Eucharist.

NOTES

Other resources available for children's ministry

Wipe-clean Let's go… series

FaithMap

I Belong Special
for children with an intellectual disability

Let's Play
Puppets tell parables

Ichthus
a weekly mass sheet for children

For more details, pricing information or to order:
PHONE: 01420 88222 | EMAIL: sales@rpbooks.co.uk | ONLINE: www.rpbooks.co.uk

This is to say that I

_____

_____

am preparing for my
FIRST HOLY COMMUNION

~

*I will do my best to attend all
the sessions, and with God's help
I will grow more like
JESUS every day.*

*God blesses the
work I am doing for my*
**FIRST
HOLY COMMUNION**

~

*Blessed be God
for ever*